A Research on China's Economic Growth Potential

After impressive growth of about 10% per annum for three decades, China's visible signs of economic slowdown since 2008 have been subject to much contention. What causes the deceleration? What should we expect in an era of China's 6% growth? This book answers these questions in three parts.

Although it is widely accepted that China can hardly continue its high-speed growth model, estimations for its future growth potential differ greatly. The first part of this book predicts China's growth to 2050, which considers both cross-country historical experiences and China's own demographic structure and employment participation features. In the second part, the book offers a comprehensive estimation of China's national and provincial total factor productivity (TFP) over the period of 1978 to 2014 based on comparable data. It then analyzes the causes of China's economic slowdown from a productivity point of view. Finally, this book correspondingly outlines policy recommendations, including supply-side structural reform and macroeconomic policy frameworks, to effectively address the issue of decline in both labor and labor productivity growth. This book will attract scholars and students of economics and China's economic studies.

Chong-en Bai is the Mansfield Freeman Chair Professor of the School of Economics and Management, Tsinghua University China. His research areas include economic institutions, public economics, economic growth and development, and China's economy.

Qiong Zhang is an Associate Professor of the School of Public Administration and Policy, Renmin University of China. Her research focuses on labor, population, and economic growth. Her research interests mainly relate to family economics and public economics.

中国金融四十人论坛书系
CHINA FINANCE 40 FORUM BOOKS

China Finance 40 Forum (CF40) is a non-governmental, non-profit and independent think tank dedicated to policy research in the fields of macro economics and finance. CF40 operates as a "40×40 club" with about 40 influential experts around the age 40.

The "China Finance 40 Forum Books" focuses on the macroeconomic and financial field with a special emphasis on financial policy studies to facilitate innovations in financial thinking and inspire breakthroughs, while building a high-end, authentic brand for think tank books with top academic quality and policy value.

The "China Finance 40 Forum Books" has published more than 50 monographs and article collections since 2009. Through its rigorous and cutting-edge research, this book series have a remarkable reputation in the industry and a broad influence overall.

A Research on China's Economic Growth Potential

Chong-en Bai
Qiong Zhang

Translated by Xiaoru Fei,
Jingjie Zhao, and Menghan Wang

Routledge
Taylor & Francis Group

LONDON AND NEW YORK

First published 2017
by Routledge
2 Park Square, Milton Park, Abingdon, Oxon OX14 4RN

and by Routledge
711 Third Avenue, New York, NY 10017

Routledge is an imprint of the Taylor & Francis Group, an informa business

British Library Cataloguing-in-Publication Data
A catalogue record for this book is available from the British
Library

Library of Congress Cataloging-in-Publication Data
A catalog record for this book has been requested

ISBN: 978-1-138-08277-9 (hbk)
ISBN: 978-1-315-11234-3 (ebk)

Typeset in Times New Roman
by Apex CoVantage, LLC

Contents

Figures

Tables

Acknowledgements

We would like to express our appreciation to the China Finance 40 Forum (CF40) and the Shanghai Finance Institute (SFI) for providing the financial support that made this study possible. We are particularly grateful for the continuing encouragement and insightful suggestions from Fang Cai of the Chinese Academy of Social Sciences, Shijin Liu of the Development Research Center of the State Council, Ruo-en Ren of Beijing University of Aeronautics and Astronautics, and Xianchun Xu of the Chinese National Bureau of Statistics. Bing Hu and Dongdong Ma of the China Finance 40 Forum and Jing Zhao of Taylor & Francis helped us with many editorial suggestions to improve the clarity of the manuscript. We also wish to thank University of Toronto alumna Xiaoru Fei and Menghan Wang and Jingjie Zhao of the China Finance 40 Forum for the translation of the manuscript.

The opinions expressed in this study are those of the authors and do not necessarily reflect the views of the China Finance 40 Forum and the Shanghai Finance Institute.

Chong-en Bai
Mansfield Freeman Chair Professor
Tsinghua University
Qiong Zhang
Associate Professor
Renmin University of China

Introduction

Chong-en Bai and Qiong Zhang

As the Chinese economy records the lowest growth rate in 2015 since 1990 and continues to face downward pressure, a clear trend toward slower expansion is now apparent. What should we expect in an "era of 6% growth"? Is the deceleration of growth in recent years the product of cyclical repercussions post-2008 financial crisis or the result of long-term structural changes? At what level will China be able to maintain its economic growth in the future? This study will strive to answer these questions in three parts: first, it will predict long-term growth potential from a supply-side perspective; second, it will discuss the sources of change in productivity in China and analyze the causes of the economic slowdown since 2008 from a productivity point of view; third, the study will offer policy advice based on the findings in the previous two parts.

The study first predicts that China's future economic growth rates will be 6.29% for 2016 to 2020, 5.54% for 2012 to 2025, 4.84% for 2026 to 2030, 3.96% for 2031 to 2035, 3.31% for 2036 to 2040, 3.33% for 2041 to 2015, and 2.90% for 2046 to 2050. As China rapidly closes the gap with the frontier economies, its advantages as a latecomer will diminish, leading to the drop in labor productivity growth. Meanwhile, slowing population growth as well as population aging will inevitably lead to shrinking labor supply, suggesting that for a relatively long period in the future China's growth potential will continue on its downward trajectory.

With regard to the determinants influencing China's efficiency of inputs to outputs, the study finds that openness enhances productivity, while regions at higher stages of development on average have lower productivity growth. Non-productive investment and the growth in the employment participation rate affect productivity growth negatively and positively, respectively, through their influence on the effective quantity of factor input. Government intervention has a significant and negative impact on productivity growth, as does the investment rate. China's recent decline in productivity growth can be largely explained by the weakening latecomer advantages and a rising investment rate. The economic growth after 2008 relied more on the sharp increase of the investment rate, hampering productivity and household consumption growth. In addition, economic stimulus measures have proven ineffectual in reversing the long-term decline in economic growth. When these measures expire, their "growth stabilizing" effects will fade, but the negative impact on productivity growth will linger on.

The study observes that the deceleration of economic growth in China is inevitable in the long run, and the country needs further reforms to prevent the growth rate from dropping too much. Based on that, it suggests that implementing cyclical policy measures to solve demand-side problems is not enough. There is also need to speed up structural reforms on the supply side to make sure the economy is developing reasonably, gradually reduce government investment as an instrument to execute demand-side management and stimulate stable growth, focus more on achieving structural balance through supply-side reforms, and improve the quality of economic growth by placing more emphasis on innovation as a key driver of growth. Moreover, the country needs a macro policy framework that can effectively tackle the drop in the growth rate of both labor force and labor productivity.

To be specific, this study recommends shifting the focus of fiscal policy from expenditure to tax reduction; reducing government intervention and strictly implementing budget regulations so the country can have better control over local debts; cutting down social security contribution rates; simplifying administrative procedures and decentralizing governance in order to enhance companies' vitality and competitiveness; investing more in people and promoting a balanced coverage of preschool and compulsory education under the guideline of "wide coverage, secured access to basic education, and guaranteed education quality" to improve labor productivity; preventing financial institutions and financial markets from channeling funds to zombie companies and promoting the survival of the fittest to reduce overcapacity; improving the compensation mechanism to contain possible social problems caused by firm exit; deepening the market system reform; abandoning the distribution model wherein the government dominates the allocation of key factors such as land and capital; relying more on market self-adjustment to optimize the distribution of capital and labor across sectors; reforming household registration policy and land policy to promote new-type urbanization; boosting labor use efficiency and reducing real estate inventory; implementing financial reforms to give financial institutions and markets more independence and ensuring more comprehensive financial supervision; punishing credit default according to the law; and improving risk monitoring and early warning. There is also need to speed up reforms in financing and investment regimes, remove the institutional basis that generates and magnifies financial risks, and promote deleveraging. Furthermore, China should remain vigilant for possible negative impacts of exchange rate reforms and take preemptive measures to avoid them, steadily promoting the internationalization of the renminbi, while retaining monetary policy independence and control over the amount of currency in circulation.

1 China's growth potential to 2050

A supply-side forecast based on cross-country productivity convergence and its featured labor force

Introduction

As downward pressure on the Chinese economy persists, a clear trend toward slower expansion has become evident. The actual growth rate was down from 2000 to 2007's annual average of 10.51% to 9.60% in 2008 and it hit the bottom in 2009 at 9.20%, after which it rebounded again. However, in 2011 the rate went down again, with 2015's growth rate falling to 6.90%, the lowest since 1990. The average annual growth rate between 2011 and 2015 was 7.82%, which was significantly lower than the 10.03% between 1978 and 2007. Growth rates during the first three quarters of 2016 were all 6.7%, during which economic downward pressure has continued to increase.[1] What should we expect from a China growing at a rate of around 6%? What is its growth projection over the short and long term? These questions have been thoroughly explored and debated by many research institutions and researchers both at home and abroad. Foreign institutions such as the International Monetary Fund, the World Bank, and the Asian Development Bank; domestic institutions such as the Mid- and Long-Term Growth Research Team at the Development Research Center of the State Council,[2] the China Economic Growth Frontline Research Team,[3] and the Forecast and Analysis of the Economic Situation Research Team[4] (both at the Chinese Academy of Social Sciences); and scholars such as Fang Cai from the Chinese Academy of Social Sciences,[5] Justin Yifu Lin from the National School of Development at Peking University, Jun Zhang from the School of Economics at Fudan University, and many others have all expressed their views on different occasions.

Although these studies have all pointed out that it is hard to continue the high-speed growth model which has been in place since the reform and opening up period began, but estimations for China's future growth potential differ greatly (we list some of the research conclusions that are representative and have considerable impact): Holz (2006) predicted China's growth rates for 2015 to 2020 and 2020 to 2025 are 5.50–10.90% and 3.98–13.51%, respectively. Wang and his colleagues (2007) predicted that China's growth rate for 2011 to 2020 is between 5.92% and 9.26%. Zhang and Lou (2009) predicted that China's growth rate for 2016 to 2020 is 6.7%, but would fall to 5.4% or even 4.5% in a pessimistic scenario. Eichengreen and his colleagues (2011) predicted that China's annual growth rates for 2011 to 2020 and 2021 to 2030 were 6.1–7.0% and 5.0–6.2%, respectively. Another research report jointly released by the Asian Development Bank and Peking University pointed out that China's average annual growth rate for 2010 to 2020 and 2020 to 2030 would be 8% and 6%, respectively; Johansson *et al.* (2012) predicted that China's average annual growth rate for 2011 to 2030 and 2030 to 2060 would be 6.6% and 2.3%, respectively. In the book *China in 2030: Building a Modernized Harmonious and Creative Society* jointly published by the World Bank and the Development Research Center of the State Council, China's growth rates for 2016 to 2020, 2021 to 2025, and 2026 to 2030 were predicted to be 7.0%, 5.9%, and 5.0%, respectively. Cai and Lu (2013a, 2013b) believed that China's growth rate for 2016 to 2020 would be 6.1%; it would rise to 6.7% if the contribution of human capital and the impacts of demographic transition on the capital formation rate, labor participation rate, and natural rate of unemployment were taken into consideration. Pritchett and Summers (2014) pointed out that China's past high-speed economic growth would "return to the mean value" and that the growth rate for 2013 to 2023 and 2023 to 2033 would fall to 5.01% and 3.28%, respectively.[6] Qu (2015) believed that China's growth rates before year 2020 would all be above 8% and 8.5% for 2015 to 2020. Lu and Cai (2016) pointed out that China's potential growth rates for 2016 to 2020, 2021 to 2015, 2026 to 2030, 2031 to 2035, 2036 to 2040, 2041 to 2045, and 2046 to 2050 would be 6.600%, 5.633%, 4.983%, 4.540%, 3.935%, 3.151%, and 2.474%, respectively. If impacts of household registration system reform, education and training system reform, SOE reform on labor participation rate, human capital, and total factor productivity (under various scenarios of the fertility rate due to different birth control policy combinations) were alternatively assumed, the growth rate would rise 1 to 2 percentage points. *The World Economic Outlook* newly released by the International Monetary Fund on October of 2016 predicted that growth rates for years between 2016 to 2021 would be 6.59%, 6.17%, 6.03%, 6.00%, 5.90%, and 5.80%, respectively.

Methodologies and data sources for these studies vary a lot and conclusions about the source of China's past economic growth as well as scenario simulation for future growth are not fully consistent. In terms of methodology, some of the researchers focus on the demand side, paying little attention to whether China has sufficient supply capacity to meet and maintain such demands. Others look at the supply-side issues, adopting either a simple comparison approach or a growth accounting approach. The simple comparison method compares China with the experience of other countries to predict its economic growth. It emphasizes the "convergence" of economic growth, assuming that different countries have similar growth potential when they are at a similar stage of development, but fails to account for demographic and institutional differences among these countries when they reach said stage. The growth accounting method emphasizes the individuality of different countries and bases the forecast of China's economic growth on its total factor productivity, capital, and labor growth. Its underlying logic and methodology is highly controversial. On one hand, it cannot avoid discussions on the specifications of productivity functions or the output elasticity of capital and labor; on the other hand, capital accumulation comes from annual increases in output, which itself is a result of the changes in total factor productivity. Although economic growth comes either from increases in factor input or improved productivity, additivity can be an outstanding issue in the calculation of their relative contribution.

There is another method that considers both the demand and supply side simultaneously. It forecasts China's economic growth by calibrating parameters within the Computable General Equilibrium (CGE) model to suit China's situation. This approach is highly effective in making short-term predictions: it focuses on the characteristics of the economic stage China has recently undergone, considering a wide range of economic indicators and kinds of possible interactions and impacts. However, the analysis process involved this method is very complicated and the conclusions are sensitive to external cyclical shocks. In addition, it has very strict model requirements when it comes to describing how the changes influence the economy as a whole. Scholars adopting this approach differ greatly in model design and parameter selection, which creates difficulties in the discussion and comparison of their conclusions, making it even more difficult to reach a convincing agreement.

Some simplified analyses build on the "convergence" assumption and cross-country evidence in analyzing China's economic growth potential, while circumventing the problems mentioned above. Among them, the ideas of Justin Yifu Lin from Peking University and Jun Zhang from Fudan University are worth mentioning. Lin points out that, in 2008, China's GDP per capita was 21% of that of the United States, a level roughly equivalent to Japan's relative GDP per capita in 1951, Singapore's in 1967, Taiwan's in 1975, and Korea's in 1977. These economies grew at an average rate of 9.2%, 8.6%, 8.3%, and 7.6%, respectively, in the following 20 years. Therefore, China's potential economic growth rate for the 20 years after 2008 should also be around 8%.[7]

In Jun Zhang's view, current GDP per capita in China is 22–23% of the United States' level. Assume the annual growth rate in the United States is 2%. Based on the function between this year's GDP per capita growth rates of Japan and Asia's Four Little Dragons (Singapore, Hong Kong, Taiwan, and Korea), and their last year's relative GDP per capita to that of the United States, China's potential GDP per capita growth rate for the following years will be 8.07% (2015), 7.94% (2016), 7.80% (2017), 7.65% (2018), 7.50% (2019), . . ., and 4.88% (2035). Taking into account a population growth rate of 0.4–0.5%, China can grow at a rate no slower than 8% during the 13th Five-Year Plan period (2016 to 2020).

In the above analysis, two aspects indicate that China might follow a grow path similar to those experienced in Japan, Singapore, Taiwan, and Korea at their respective comparable stages: in recent years, the investment rate in China is significantly higher than those in Japan, Taiwan, and Korea when they were undergoing a similar stage of development, but lower than that of Singapore (Figure 1.1, left part);[8] China's human capital level is markedly higher than that of Singapore at a comparable stage, but similar to that of Japan, Taiwan, and Korea (Figure 1.1, right part).

Meanwhile, another two very important phenomena have not received enough attention. At a comparable stage, Japan and the Four Little Dragons of Asia witnessed a continued decline (the window of demographic opportunity known as the "demographic dividend") in total dependency ratio

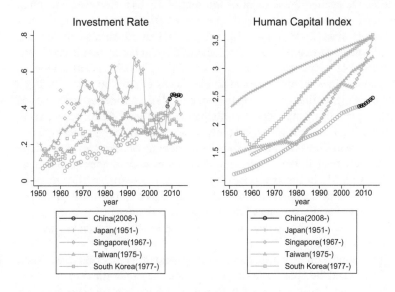

Figure 1.1 Similarities between China and other East Asian economies

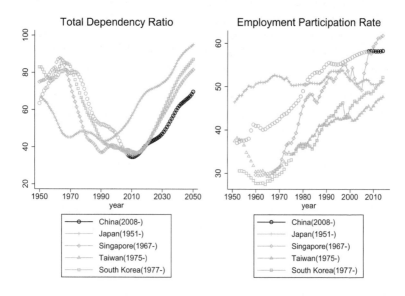

Figure 1.2 Differences between China and other East Asian economies

(the ratio of the number of children aged 0–14 plus elderly people aged 65 and above against the amount of those aged 15–64). However, in China, the total dependency ratio has been rising swiftly instead of dropping significantly since 2008 (Figure 1.2, left part).[9] Other than that, the current employment participation rate (the ratio of the number of people employed to the whole population) in China (nearly 60%) is much higher than that of Singapore, Taiwan, and Korea at similar levels of development (30–35%) and even higher than that of Japan (around 45%). Considering the trends of these economies' employment participation rates over the following years (Figure 1.2, right part), we can hardly believe that the employment participation rate in China has much room for further growth. The two phenomena are closely related, both suggesting that, compared with these economies, China's past high-speed economic growth can be partly attributed to its more favorable demographic structure and higher employment participation. They also indicate that China may perform significantly worse in terms of economic catching up than these economies at similar development periods in the future.

Interestingly, in exploring the similarities and differences between China and Japan and the Four Little Dragons of Asia, the similarities in investment rate (or capital deepening) and human capital influence the level of output per unit of labor force (or labor productivity), whereas the differences in demographic structure and employment participation mainly affect the size of labor force in an economy. Moreover, past research shows that labor productivity as an indicator is not only simple and straightforward, but also helps to avoid discussions about the specific forms of production functions or input-output elasticity. The labor force is affected by population age structure and labor participation, which are largely specific to a country's social and economic environment and insusceptible to the influence of other domestic or foreign factors. This is the logical starting point for our following projections of China's future economic growth. We hypothesize and show through analysis that cross-country convergence is mainly manifested in labor productivity changes, while the demographic factors exhibit patterns particular to each country's own socioeconomic development.

Analysis framework and methodology

We first portray the patterns of cross-country growth based on historical data (see Figure 1.3). The data in our analysis came from Maddison (2010) due to two considerations:[10] first this database covers a long period of time (AD1 to AD2008) and has been frequently used in international historical comparisons. Second, scholars such as Justin Yifu Lin (as mentioned previously) also used this database in research, which we will use as a reference. Furthermore, the analytical framework we later used came from Lucas

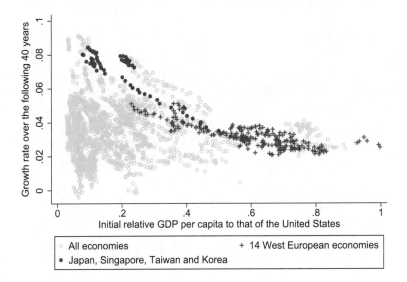

Figure 1.3 Cross-country economic growth patterns

(2009), and Lucas used the same database. Adopting the same data source helps us to compare our conclusions with the existing ones. As Figure 1.3 shows, economies with lower initial levels of per capita GDP relative to that of the United States tend to grow on average at faster rates in the following 40 years. The four East Asian economies (Japan, Singapore, Taiwan, and Korea), and the 14 West European economies we selected display relatively good catching-up performance.[11]

Next, we decompose the convergence patterns into GDP per capita growth and total population growth (Figure 1.4). In Figure 1.4, the pair-wise relationship between relative GDP per capita for any economy to that of the United States for each year from 1950 to 1968 and average growth rate of GDP per capita (the left part of Figure 1.4) or total population (the right part) over the following 40 years is shown in scattered grey circles;[12] whereas that for the 14 West European economies and that for the four East Asian economies (Japan, Singapore, Taiwan, and Korea) are highlighted in solid circles, respectively. Comparing Figure 1.4 to Figure 1.3, we find that cross-country growth convergence is mainly a convergence of GDP per capita instead of a convergence of total population.

We go on to break down the convergence patterns into labor productivity (GDP per unit of labor input) and labor force (Figure 1.5).[13] Similarly, we here show the pairwise relationship between relative labor productivity for

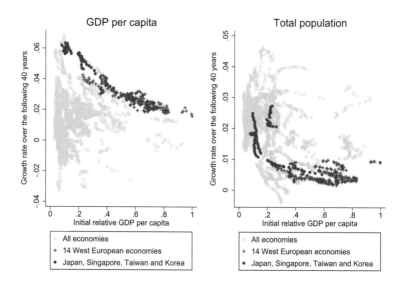

Figure 1.4 Breakdown of cross-country growth convergence (GDP per capita and total population)

any economy to that of the United States for each year from 1950 to 1968 and average growth rate of labor productivity (the left part of Figure 1.4) or total labor force (the right part) over the following 40 years with scattered grey circles.[14] Those for the 14 West European economies and the four East Asian economies are also respectively highlighted in solid circles for emphasis. Comparing Figure 1.5 to Figures 1.3 and 1.4, we can see a stronger convergence in labor productivity. In addition, the four East Asian economies (Japan, Singapore, Taiwan, and Korea) and 14 West European economies have demonstrated very similar convergence patterns. The 18 economies together form the growth frontier of the development stages (relative to the labor productivity in the United States)[15]: the lower the initial labor productivity, the greater its growth potential. This feature of relative convergence in labor productivity is the most important determinant of the relative convergence of cross-country economic growth. As for labor force, there isn't any apparent sign that less-developed economies have greater growth potential. The fact that the four East Asian economies outperform their West European counterparts can be attributed to the rapid growth in labor productivity as a result of catching up and the significant increase in labor force brought about by factors such as demographic dividend. When the effect of demographic dividend is removed, the two groups of economies grow at a similar pace and there seems to be no so-called East Asia Growth Miracle.

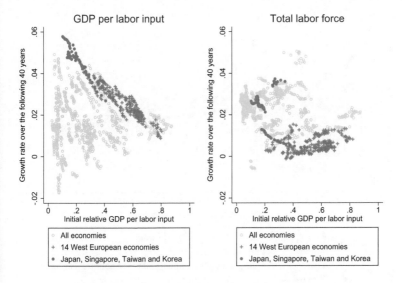

Figure 1.5 Breakdown of cross-country growth convergence (GDP per labor input and labor force)

Furthermore, according to relative convergence-related researches, since spillover and learning-based catch-up effect means that underdeveloped economies have more growth potential than developed economies, we draw on the rules of economic convergence recommended by Lucas (2009) to describe data patterns shown in Figure 1.5.[16] The rule can be described by:

$$\text{potential labor productivity growth rate for an economy}_t = \mu \left(\frac{\text{labor productivity in the United States}_{t-1}}{\text{labor productivity in the economy}_{t-1}} \right)^{\theta},$$

where μ and θ are both parameters to be estimated, of which the former represents the growth rate of GDP per labor force in the United States and the latter the speed of convergence of labor productivity for the said economy to that of the United States.

We first choose economies (including West European and East Asian economies) with levels of labor productivity (relative to that of the United States) comparable to that of China in 2008 (approximately 17% of that of the United States) as points of reference.[17] We then use a non-linear Gauss-Newton iterative method to estimate the parameters μ and θ directly (results can be found in Figure 1.6). Since the size of an economy may affect its speed of convergence to the frontier economy (the United States), we have

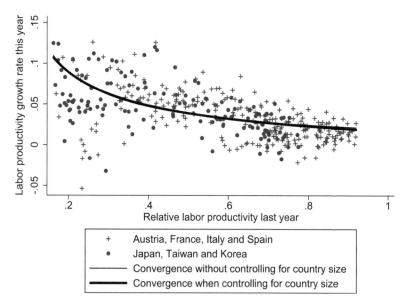

Figure 1.6 Convergence of labor productivity (referent economies)

also included results when controlling for "country size" as measured by total population in Figure 1.6.

Figure 1.6 further shows that the four West European economies (Austria, France, Italy, and Spain) exhibit patterns of labor productivity convergence to the United States similar to those of the three East Asian economies (Japan, Taiwan, and Korea) in comparable development stages. Moreover, country size has no influence on cross-country labor productivity convergence.

Therefore, in later analysis, we will only use the three East Asian economies (Japan, Taiwan, and Korea) as references, and exclude the impact of country size on the convergence pattern of labor productivity,[18] to predict China's future labor productivity growth rates. We will base our predictions of population growth rate and employment participation rate on the characteristics of China's demographic structure and employment participation, respectively. We then predict each year's labor force growth using previously mentioned data. Adding all the data together, we can obtain the future economic growth rate in China.[19] Our analysis process is as follows:

> Economic growth rate = GDP per labor input growth rate
> + labor force growth rate
> = GDP per labor input growth rate
> + population growth rate
> + change in employment participation rate

In addition, in the analysis, as a response to topical issues such as "is the current slowing down of China's economic growth the result of post-crisis cyclical fluctuation or long-term structural deceleration?" and "what are the effects of China and the United States' economic stimulus plans?", we will predict China's economic growth in two scenarios. In the first scenario, we set the starting point of our projection at 2014. Between 2008 and 2014, China's economic performance was consistently better than the actual performance of the United States, meaning that China's economic development level is fast approaching that of the United States and therefore there is less room for catching up. In the second scenario, the beginning point is set at 2008, ignoring the difference in economic performance in the two countries after 2008. Although we tend to believe that the first scenario is closer to reality, we cannot rule out the second, given that China's "ultra-good" performance resulting from the stimulus plan might have exacerbated the existing distortion in its economy and caused a "fault-like" reverse as the positive effects of the stimulus fade, thus widening the distance from the United States (returning to 2008's relative level).

Data source and growth forecast

As aforementioned, we will estimate China's labor productivity growth rate and labor force growth rate, and then add them together to arrive at the economic growth rate for each year. Moreover, for labor productivity growth rate, we are going to set 2008 and 2014 as the respective starting points in our simulation, so as to distinguish between the short-term cyclical and long-term structural impact of China's post-crisis stimulus measures.

1) Forecasting labor productivity growth rate

Specifically, for labor productivity (GDP per labor input), we apply a non-linear Gauss-Newton iterative approach to the cross-country data drawn from Maddison (2010) and PWT9.0 to plot the growth trajectory of China's potential labor productivity[20]; based on this, we calculate its annual growth rate of labor productivity in future years. The results are shown in Figure 1.7.

For comparison, we have also included in Figure 1.7 the relation between China's actual growth rate of GDP per labor input in each year since 1978 against its relative labor productivity to that of the United States in the previous year. The left part of Figure 1.7 shows estimates based on data

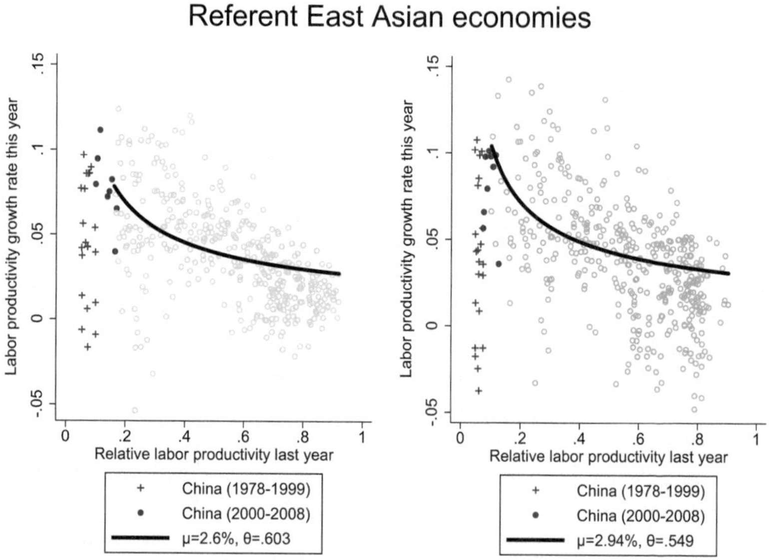

Figure 1.7 Growth pattern of China's labor productivity

from Maddison (the parameters μ and θ are estimated to be 2.60% and 0.60, respectively).[21] The results indicate that although the convergence of China's labor productivity in early years (1978 to 1999) diverged from that of the aforementioned East Asian economies (compared with those economies, China's actual labor productivity growth rates were lower than the estimated figures at comparable stages); its convergence pattern is highly similar in recent years (2000 to 2008). The right part of Figure 1.7 displays results based on data from PWT9.0 analyzed in similar approaches. The conclusion is consistent.

Based on these findings, we will iterate the (potential) growth rate of China's labor productivity from 2009 to 2050 (setting 2008 as the starting point for iteration) and from 2015 to 2050 (2014 as the starting point), according to the growth pattern of labor productivity of the three referent East Asian economies in comparable stages of development as shown in Figure 1.7.[22] Results for the two situations are shown in the left and right parts of Figure 1.8, respectively. In Figure 1.8, we have also included China's actual labor productivity growth rates based on data from Maddison (2010) and PWT9.0.

Table 1.1 first lists both the estimated and actual annual labor productivity growth rates for years 2009 to 2015.[23] We discover that between 2009 and 2011, the actual rates are significantly higher than the mean of the

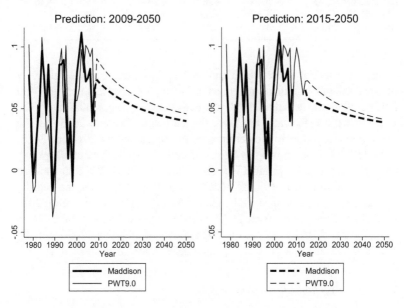

Figure 1.8 Labor productivity growth rate in China from 1978 to 2050

Table 1.1 Labor productivity growth rates (%) in China from 2009 to 2015

	Estimated level		Actual figure
	Maddison	PWT9.0	NBS
2009	7.35	9.04	9.05
2010	7.15	8.76	10.23
2011	6.97	8.50	9.09
2012	6.79	8.26	7.53
2013	6.63	8.03	7.44
2014	6.48	7.82	6.94
2015	6.34	7.63	6.64

Table 1.2 (Potential) labor productivity growth rates in China from 2016 to 2050

	Simulation interval 2009–2050			Simulation interval 2016–2050		
	Maddison	PWT9.0	Average	Maddison	PWT9.0	Average
2016	6.20	7.44	6.82	5.71	7.05	6.38
2016–2020	5.96	7.12	6.54	5.51	6.70	6.11
2021–2025	5.44	6.43	5.94	5.09	5.97	5.53
2026–2030	5.04	5.90	5.47	4.76	5.42	5.09
2031–2035	4.71	5.48	5.10	4.48	5.00	4.74
2036–2040	4.45	5.15	4.80	4.26	4.66	4.46
2041–2045	4.22	4.87	4.55	4.07	4.39	4.23
2046–2050	4.04	4.64	4.34	3.90	4.16	4.03

estimated potential rates, which can be largely ascribed to the relatively strong economic stimulus implemented in China during this period. From 2012 to 2014, the actual rates fall just between the two potential rates. The actual and estimated rates are close for the years 2012 and 2013, but the actual rate is significantly lower than the estimated rate for 2014 and 2015.

Table 1.2 further shows the estimated results for the (potential) growth rate of China's labor productivity from 2016 to 2050. We estimate that the potential rate will be 6.38%–6.82% in 2016 and then decline year by year as China catches up with the United States: 6.11%–6.54% from 2016 to 2020, 5.53%–5.94% from 2021 to 2015, 5.09%–5.47% from 2026 to 2030, 4.74%–5.10% from 2031 to 2035, 4.46%–4.80% from 2036 to 2040, 4.23%–4.55% from 2041 to 2045, and 4.03%–4.34% from 2046 to 2050.

2) Forecasting labor force growth rate

Now, we are going to consider the growth of labor force in China in future years. As is mentioned above, the breakdown of cross-country growth convergence shows that unlike labor productivity growth, labor force growth does not present a relative convergence pattern. After 2008, there is a notable difference between China and the referent East Asian economies at their respective comparable stages of development. China entered into the population-aging period when the total dependence ratio started to rise instead of fall around 2010, when the referent economies were still experiencing a rise in employment participation rate. China's employment participation rate had already far surpassed those of the referent economies around 2008, thus leaving little room for growth in the future. Therefore, the labor force growth patterns seen in these East Asian economies cannot provide any reference for the forecast of China's future labor force growth. We need to rely on China's own characteristics to make predictions.

Taking into consideration both relevant theoretical predictions and data availability, we separate labor force growth rate into two parts – population growth rate and employment participation growth rate – in our estimation. The population growth rate is estimated as follows. First, we use the total population estimates for China between 2015 and 2050 from *The World Population Prospects: 2015 Revision* to calculate the annual population growth rates. The results are shown in Figure 1.9.[24]

In Figure 1.9, we display the official data of "total population" in China covering the period 1959 to 2014 from the NBS website, the estimated

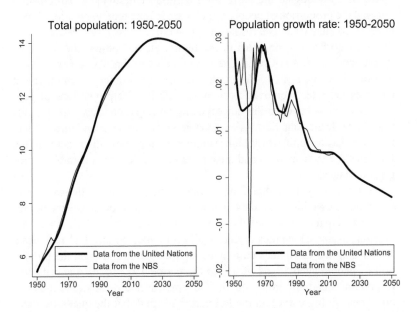

Figure 1.9 Total population and population growth rate in China between 1950 and 2050

"total population" from *The World Population Prospects: 2015 Revision* (left part of Figure 1.9), and the corresponding "population growth rate" (right part of Figure 1.9). We find that the "total population" data given by *The World Population Prospects: 2015 Revision* are slightly below those from the NBS in most of the years. Additionally, the "population growth rate" obtained based on the NBS data fluctuates less than those calculated based on data from *The World Population Prospects: 2015 Revision* before 1970, but more after 1970.

Next we predict the growth rate of China's employment participation rate in future years. We believe that while the employment participation rate, or the proportion of employed population among total population, is affected by cyclical unemployment caused by economic fluctuation, the most important determinants are the share of the working-age population (15–64 years old) in total population and the willingness to work influenced by Chinese cultural and institutional background, which typically changes very slowly and thus can be assumed to remain fixed. Therefore, we base our estimation of China's future employment participation rate on the correlation between the employment participation rate and the percentage of people aged 15–64 among total population as shown in the data, as well as on the estimates of the proportion of people aged 15–64 among total population between 2015 and 2050 from *The World Population Prospects: 2015 Revision*.[25]

We first investigate the correlation between employment participation rate and the proportion of people aged 15–64 among total population shown in cross-country data. The results are shown in Figure 1.10.[26] We compare three categories of economies in the figure: all economies, the four East Asian economies, and China. The figure indicates that the larger the proportion of people aged 15–64 in an economy, the higher the employment participation rate. Moreover, economies with similar proportions of people aged 15–64 have similar employment participation rates, which holds true for both the four East Asian economies and other economies. China, however, has a significantly higher employment participation rate than the four East Asian economies and most other economies at comparable demographic stages.

As such, we will predict China's future employment participation rate based on its own historical data, instead of the correlation between employment participation rate and the proportion of people aged 15–64 of the four East Asian economies or that of all economies. Figure 1.11 includes a scatter diagram of China's employment participation rates and the proportion of people aged 15–64 years for the period 1952 to 2014 and its corresponding quadratic fitting curve (the simplest and most straightforward non-linear fitting curve) on the left part.[27] We find that the quadratic function we get based on the proportion of people aged 15–64 can very well

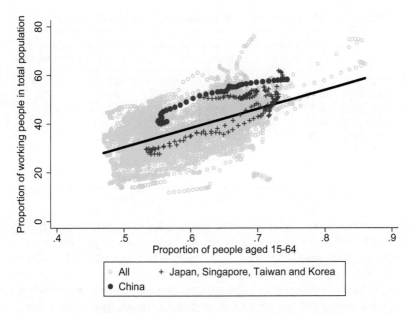

Figure 1.10 Correlation between employment participation rate and the proportion of people aged 15–64

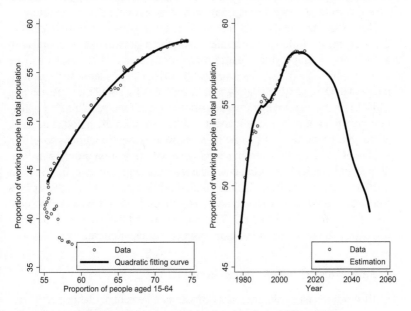

Figure 1.11 China's employment participation rate from 1978 to 2050

Table 1.3 China's labor force growth rate and breakdown from 2016 to 2050

	Labor force growth rate (%)	Among it: population growth rate	Among it: employment participation growth rate
2016	0.31	0.46	−0.15
2016–2020	0.18	0.39	−0.21
2021–2025	0.00	0.17	−0.16
2026–2030	−0.25	0.00	−0.26
2031–2035	−0.79	−0.10	−0.68
2036–2040	−1.15	−0.19	−0.96
2041–2045	−0.90	−0.29	−0.61
2046–2050	−1.14	−0.39	−0.75

reflect the change of employment participation rates in China from 1978 to 2014. Therefore, we compute the employment participation rates from 2015 to 2050 based on this quadratic function and the estimated proportion of people aged 15–64 in future years (results are shown in the right part of Figure 1.11). Figure 1.11 shows that China entered its population-aging period around 2010 as the total dependency ratio that used to be declining continuously in the "demographic dividend" period began to rise. Furthermore, it will face increasingly more severe population aging, suggesting that the proportion of people aged 15–64 will continue to drop in the future. This in turn indicates lower employment participation rates in the future.

Next, we estimate China's annual labor force growth rate from 2016 to 2050 using the following formula: labor force growth rate = population growth rate + employment participation growth rate. The results can be seen in Table 1.3. Table 1.3 shows that in 2016, China's labor force growth rate was 0.31%, of which 0.46% was contributed by population growth rate and -0.15% by employment participation growth rate. As China's population growth continues to slow down and the aging problem becomes more acute (the proportion of people aged between 15–64 continues to drop), total population growth rate and employment participation growth rate both drop sharply, quickly pushing down the labor force growth rate: 0.18% from 2016 to 2020, 0.00% from 2021 to 2025, -0.25% from 2026 to 2030, -0.79% from 2031 to 2035, -1.15% from 2036 to 2040, -0.90% from 2041 to 2045, and -1.14% from 2046 to 2050. The main source of the decline in the labor force growth rate is the fall of employment participation rate.

3) Forecasting economic growth rate

Until now, we have obtained data of China's (potential) labor productivity growth rate and the labor force growth rate based on the shared cross-country convergence patterns and China's distinct demographic structure

Table 1.4 (Potential) economic growth rate in China from 2016 to 2050

	Maddison	PWT9.0	Average
2016	6.01	7.35	6.68
2016–2020	5.69	6.88	6.29
2021–2025	5.10	5.97	5.54
2026–2030	4.50	5.17	4.84
2031–2035	3.70	4.21	3.96
2036–2040	3.10	3.51	3.31
2041–2045	3.17	3.49	3.33
2046–2050	2.77	3.03	2.90

and employment participation characteristics, respectively. We can combine them to yield each year's (potential) economic growth rate. The results are shown in Table 1.4.

The results in Table 1.4 show that China's potential economic growth rate in 2016 is estimated to be 6.68% (6.01–7.35%). As the growth rate of labor productivity fall progressively and the size of the labor force continues to shrink, China's annual potential economic growth rate declines continuously and goes down faster than potential labor productivity growth rate. We predict China's potential economic growth rates in the future to be 6.29% (5.69–6.88%) between 2016 and 2020, 5.54% (5.10–5.97%) between 2021 and 2025, 4.84% (4.50–5.17%) between 2026 and 2030, 3.96% (3.70–4.21%) between 2031 and 2035, 3.31% (3.10–3.51%) between 2036 and 2040, 3.33% (3.17–3.49%) between 2041 and 2045, and 2.90% (2.77–3.03%) between 2046 and 2050.

Is it likely that growth potential has been underestimated?

Two views believe that our previous analysis might have underestimated China's potential growth rate. One view is based on the institutional environment's room for improvement; the other is based on overcapacity. We will discuss these two views respectively and explain that the institutional environment's huge room for improvement and the severe overcapacity issue do not necessarily stand for a higher potential growth rate in China.

1) Impact of the institutional environment's room for improvement on potential growth rate

The view based on the institutional environment's room for improvement holds that there is still enough room for improvement for China's institutional environment and that our previous prediction did not take this situation into consideration. Thus, we underestimated China's potential growth rate.

We shall introduce a mathematical expression to address this view. We assume that the potential economic growth rate of an economy is $g(a, q)$, where a stands for the rate for institutional improvement and q is institutional quality after the improvement.

To be more accurate, q is the quality of the frontier institution corresponding to the development stage of the economy and a is the relative disparity of institutional improvement rates with other economies during their convergence with the frontier economies at the same development stage. Our previous predictions assumed that China's institutional environment has reached the frontier level of q^* corresponding to China's current economic development stage and that the improvement rate of the quality of China's institution was the same as that of those successful economies that we referred to at the same development stage; our predicted value is $g(a, q^*)$ by using this mathematical expression.

If we assume that China's institutional environment has not reached such a level, then whether the potential growth rate would be higher or not depends on what hypothesis we make about the improvement rate for institutional quality. We shall first consider two extreme situations. First, institutional quality can be improved at once and it can reach the frontier level of China's current economic development stage. If that is the case, China can not only enjoy growth brought by institutional improvement, but can enjoy the high growth potential under the institution immediately as well. Superposition of the two will be higher than our predicted value. By using our mathematical expression, China's potential growth rate would be $g(a^*, q^*)$, greater than $g(0, q^*)$. Another extreme situation is its institutions will not be improved. Under this circumstance, potential growth rate would be $g(a, q')$, in which $q' < q^*$, and this rate is below our predicted value $g(0, q^*)$.

Whether our previous analysis has underestimated China's potential growth rate depends on the speed for China's future institutional improvement; if we predict that the speed for China's institutional improvement is fast, then we have underestimated China's potential growth rate, and vice versa. More strictly speaking, whether our previous analysis has underestimated China's potential growth rate depends on the rate of China's institutional quality improvement towards that of the frontier institution and the relative speed of institutional improvement compared with the referent countries at the comparable stage: if we predict that China's institutional improvement speed is much faster than that of the successful economies that we referred to at their corresponding historical stage, then we would have underestimated China's potential growth rate, and vice versa. We certainly hope that China can improve the quality of its institutions at a faster speed so as to achieve a higher economic growth rate; however, we lack a strong basis to support such an assumption.

2) Impacts of overcapacity on the potential growth rate

The view based on overcapacity holds that China's overcapacity problem is serious at present, which reflects that aggregate demand is insufficient. Our previous prediction took only supply capacity into consideration. If China's aggregate demand could be increased, and at the same time an increase in supply capacity can be unaffected, then China can achieve a faster economic growth than our prediction in which only supply capacity was taken into account.

We believe that overcapacity does not necessarily stand for a higher potential growth rate. China's overcapacity is special: apart from overcapacity, labor cost increases rapidly and capital cost is also very high. At the same time, unemployment is not a serious problem. This indicates that China's input surplus problem was not caused by downward rigid constraints on factor prices; thus it is not a problem of insufficient aggregate demand. The problem is that China's existing capacity structure does not match its demand structure and there are frictions in capacity structure adjustments, resulting in the problem of overcapacity in certain industries.

To make things clearer, we shall use a simple two-sector model. We assume the first sector to be the new industry and the second sector the old industry. Assuming that the two sectors only use one factor (that is, capital input, K), production functions of the two sectors are respectively $Y_i = A_i f(K_i)$, where A_i is the total factor productivity in industry i ($i = 1, 2$). We assume full use of capital inputs, which indicates $K_1 + K_2 = K$. We mark initial resource allocation as $A^0 = \left(K_1^0, K_2^0, Y_1^0, Y_2^0\right)$, which locates somewhere on the production possibility frontier. When assuming the social demand preference is fixed and there are no frictions in structural adjustment, the optimal resources allocation should be $A^* = \left(K_1^*, K_2^*, Y_1^*, Y_2^*\right)$ on the production possibility frontier, in which $K_1^* > K_1^0$, $K_2^* < K_2^0$, $K_1^* + K_2^* = K_1^0 + K_2^0 = K$, $Y_1^* = A_1 f\left(K_1^*\right) > Y_1^0 = A_1 f\left(K_1^0\right)$, $Y_2^* = A_2 f\left(K_2^*\right) < Y_2^0 = A_2 f\left(K_2^0\right)$. That is to say, the social demand preference requires expansion in the new industry and scaling down in the old industry.

However, there will be frictions in structural adjustment. The adjustment process from A^0 to A^* means shift of inputs originally used in the old industry to the new industry. Losses of inputs, however, will happen during such a shift. We assume the losses rate to be a constant that is greater than 0 and less than 1. In this case, A^* cannot be achieved. Obviously, if $MPK_2 / (1 - \delta) \geq MPK_1 > MPK_2$ (where MPK_i is the marginal product of capital in industry i)

holds at A^0, the optimal resource allocation is still A^0; whereas if MPK_2 / $(1-\delta) < MPK_1$ holds at A^0, the optimal resource allocation is $A' = \left(K_1', K_2', Y_1', Y_2' \right)$, where $K_1' > K_1^0$, $K_2' < K_2^0$, $K_1' + K_2' = K_1^0 + (1-\delta)\left(K_2^0 - K_2' \right) + K_2' < K$, $Y_1' = A_1 f\left(K_1' \right) > Y_1^0$, $Y_2' = A_2 f\left(K_2' \right) < Y_2^0$, and social welfare brought by A' will be greater than that by A^0. Under this circumstance, marginal product of capital in the old industry (MPK_2) is both lower than that in the new industry (MPK_1) for the optimal resource allocation either A^0 or A', of which the latter one equals to market price of capital. That is, the marginal product of capital in the old industry is lower than its market price, indicating an overcapacity problem in that industry, whereas such a problem does not exist in the new industry.

When the optimal resource allocation is $A', K_1' + K_2' < K$, the optimal resource allocation is below the production possibility frontier when assuming no frictions; this seems to imply insufficient aggregate demand. One may expect more effective allocation, which implies more aggregate demand through realizing A^0 once again by increasing demand for the old industry through policy intervention. According to our definition, however, A' is the optimal resource allocation under such circumstance. Thus, social welfare will decline when returning A' to A^0 through policy intervention.

It is worth mentioning that calculations of GDP depend on the choice of relative prices. Apart from its impacts on resource allocation, policy intervention also exerts impacts on relative prices. If we use the relative prices after intervention as base prices when calculating GDP, GDP will be increased from A' to A^0. However, the goal of economic development should be the pursuit of social welfare improvement rather than GDP growth. Thus, the above-mentioned intervention should not be carried out. If there are no interventions, overcapacity does not indicate greater potential in GDP growth.

If we further assume the productivity A_1 in the new industry will increase in the future along with its expanded production scale – that is to say, there is a "learning-by-doing" effect in the new industry whereas such effect does not exist in the old industry – we can prove that the optimal resource allocation might no longer be A^0 as well even if $MPK_2 / (1 - \delta) \geq MPK_1 > MPK_2$ holds. Under such circumstances, the new industry scale should be expanded and the old reduced. The government should not use policy interventions to increase demand for the old industry, as it may not only reduce the current social welfare, but also reduce future growth potential and social welfare level.

Conclusion

In conclusion, the Chinese economy has exhibited a clear slowdown in its economic development. Is it a manifestation of cyclical impacts in the post-crisis era or an economic new normal as China enters a period featuring mid- to high-speed growth? What about China's future growth potential? These topics have drawn much attention and the conclusions carry important policy implications. Current discussions mainly adopt the following three approaches: estimating China's future economic growth rate based on predictions of its future demand growth; comparing China's economic growth rate with other countries at similar development stages; and calculating China's future economic growth rate using projections of future productivity development and input growth within a growth accounting framework. The first approach focuses on the demand side, while the other two pay more attention to the supply side.

Our focus is still on the supply side. The method we use, however, will be somewhere in between the two supply-side approaches mentioned above: we forecast China's future economic growth from two perspectives – labor productivity growth and changes in labor force. Based on the frequently used cross-country data from Maddison (2010) and the Penn World Table (PWT9.0), we found that labor productivity shows relatively strong convergence regularity: upon reaching a certain stage of economic development, the more-developed economy begins to have a slower labor productivity growth rate. However, no regular relation between labor force growth and economic development was found. We therefore used the cross-country convergence rules of labor productivity to forecast the growth in China's future labor productivity, whereas we gave full considerations of China's demographic structure and employment participation features when predicting its labor force growth. Such a method bypasses discussions about the forms of production function, effectively reducing controversies. Meanwhile, we used the year 2008 and the year 2014, respectively, as the start point of the projection, and simulated and predicted China's economic growth for each year over 2016 to 2050. We found that the Chinese economy outperformed the United States economy during 2008 to 2015, which narrowed the gap between China and the United States. The reduced room for "catching up" in the future will lead to a lower economic growth potential.

Our prediction shows that China's potential economic growth rate will decrease year by year during 2016 to 2050: it will drop to a level around 6.29% during 2016 to 2020, around 5.54% during 2021 to 2025, around 4.84% during 2026 to 2030, around 3.96% during 2013 to 2035, around 3.31% during 2036 to 2040, around 3.33% during 2041 to 2056, and around 2.90% during 2046 to 2050. As China rapidly closes up the distance to the frontier economies, its latecomer advantages naturally decrease, leading to continuous declines in labor productivity growth. At the same time, the slowing population growth and increasingly severe population-aging problem, as well as the shrinking of its labor force, mean that a decreasing economic growth potential will be an inevitable trend for China over a long period of time.

It is worth mentioning that in the current analysis, we did not factor in the impacts of "universal two-child policy" and other possible changes in China's childbearing policy on its total population and demographic structure, or its short-term impacts (female workers exit the labor market due to childbearing) and long-term impacts (increase in working-age population) on the labor market. We also did not factor in the impacts of the extension of the retirement age, another topical issue that affects employment participation rate. All these issues and other topics will be our focus in the future.

Notes

1 "Growth rate" data here is calculated based on annual (1978 to 2014) and quarterly (2015 to 2016) data of "gross domestic product (GDP) index (previous year=100)" from the Chinese National Bureau of Statistics (NBS for short hereafter) website.
2 Refer to various issues of *China's Economic Outlook in Ten Years* compiled by Shijin Liu (2013 to 2022 "Looking for the New Driving Force and the Balance," 2014 to 2023 "New Normal of Growth in Reform, 2015 to 2024 "Scale the Highland of Efficiency," which are published by China CITIC Press in 2013, 2014, and 2015, respectively).
3 Refer to the articles by the research group published on the *Economic Research Journal* (*Jingji Yanjiu* in Chinese), such as *Expansion and Capitalization and Catching-up Economy Technological Advancements* (Issue 5, 2010), *China's Economic Growth Path, Efficiency and Potential Growth* (Issue 11, 2012), and *Low Efficiency Impacts of China's Economic Growth and Slow Down* (Issue 12, 2014).
4 Refer to various issues of *Economic Blue Books* by the research group (2013, 2014, 2015, 2016), which are published by Social Sciences Academic Press in 2012, 2013, 2014, and 2015, respectively.
5 Cai (2016) offered a great review on relevant researches.
6 The article assumed that China's population growth rate at that period was 0; thus, the predicted value of economic growth rate was the predicted value of per capita GDP growth rate.
7 See the speech delivered by Lin at the 110th anniversary of the Nanjing Agriculture University (September 18, 2012) and the article published thereafter in the Financial Times (March 6, 2014).
8 Figures are sourced from the newly released Penn World Table (PWT9.0). More details about this source and its previous updates can be found in Feenstra *et al.* (2015).
9 This is computed based on the estimates for 1950 to 2015 and the medium-fertility variant projection for 2015 to 2050 in *The World Population Prospects: 2015 Revision* released by the United Nations Department of Economic and Social Affairs Population Division. The total dependency ratio (TDR for short) is the sum of child dependency ratio (CDR for short, defined as population aged 0–14 divided by population aged 15–64) and old dependency ratio (ODR for short, defined as population aged 65 and above divided by population aged 15–64). It measures the average number of children and aged dependents to each working-age person aged 15–64. Since not every person aged 15–64 is

employed and some of those aged 0–14 and 65 and above may be in the labor force, the total dependency ratio is in fact an "age dependency ratio," which is closely related to but not the same as the "economic dependency ratio."

10 Data source: www.ggdc.net/MADDISON/oriindex.htm. We cite it as Maddison (2010) as the data set we use is the last version of the Angus Maddison homepage, last updated in March 2010.

11 Here the analysis interval covers 1950 to 2008. The 14 West European economies are: Ireland, Austria, Belgium, Denmark, Finland, France, Germany, Italy, Holland, Norway, Sweden, Switzerland, Britain, and Spain (hereafter the same list of countries). We draw on Lucas's (2009) research (published in the *American Economic Journal*), but our research is slightly different from his. Lucas chose the data for 1960 and 2000 from Maddison (2003) and based his research on the conclusions of Sachs and Warner (1995), who selected 17 West European economies (the above-mentioned 14 economies plus Greece, Portugal, and the combination of 13 small West European countries) to observe (long-term) economic growth patterns. Our research data here come from the latest edition of Maddison's data (2010) and we think that, compared with the above 14 West European economies, Greece and Portugal had poorer performance at similar development stages and the 13 small West European countries are not one specific country or region (part of the data needed in our following analysis comes from different data sources and do not necessarily cover all the 13 small West European countries). We therefore have excluded these three economies and focused on the other 14 economies in our following analysis.

12 The analysis here covers 1950 to 2008, of which the data is from Maddison (2010).

13 The interval here is 1950 to 2008. The "labor productivity" in the figure is defined as the ratio of GDP to labor force, representing the output level of per unit labor force. The GDP data comes from Maddison (2010); labor force data are from PWT9.0. The interval for PWT9.0 data is 1960 to 2011 and that for Maddison (2010) is AD1 to AD2008. In the following analysis, if we need labor force data before 1950, we use the following method to estimate: we find that data of "employment participation rate (the number of people employed per 100 people)" in the above-mentioned 14 West European economies, Japan, and the United States in 1950, 1973, 1990, and 1998 from Maddison (2003) is very similar to the estimates of "employment participation rate" ("number of people employed" against "total population") in PWT9.0 (correlation coefficient: 0.998). Therefore, we use linear interpolation to supplement the missing data for 1870 to 1950 and estimate the number of employed population for 1870 to 1950 based on the total population data provided by Maddison (2010).

14 The analysis here covers 1950 to 2008, of which the data is from Maddison (2010).

15 We have also considered different scenarios in which we take five years, 10 years, 20 years, and 30 years as analysis intervals. The results are similar to those when we take 40 years as an interval.

16 Lucas (2009) focuses actually on (long-term) convergence of economic growth. He also points out that at early stages of economic development, the growth rate may increase as the economy develops (thus economic growth diverges instead of converges). We believe that China has already passed that stage and therefore considers only the convergence features. In addition, to project China's future economic growth for individual years, we narrowed the 40-years interval in

the convergence estimation framework adopted in Lucas (2009) to a one-year interval.

17 We set the starting point of our prediction in 2008 for two reasons: first, Maddison (2010) has data until 2008; second, the economic crisis after 2008 has cyclical impact on China and other economies. The GDP per labor input in China in 2008 is around 17% of that in the United States, approximately the same level as Japan in 1948, Taiwan in 1965, and Korea in 1968 (Singapore has never reached China's 2008 level). It is also similar to Austria's level in 1947, France's in 1945, Italy's in 1946, and Spain's in 1946. Therefore, our sample of East Asian economies covers Japan (1945–), Taiwan (1965–), and Korea (1968–) and our sample of West European economies cover Austria (1947–), France (1945–), Italy (1946–), and Spain (1946–).

18 We did not consider the four West European economies. This is because, on one hand, their social and economic situation is vastly different from that of China; on the other hand, although their GDP per labor input against that of the United States in the period 1945 to 1947 were around the same level as that of China in 2008, the years 1945 to 1947 were around the period when their GDP per labor input against that of the United States plummeted and rebounded. This is different from the situation in Taiwan and Korea from the 1960s to 1970s, when their GDP per labor input took up a similar proportion of the United States' to that of China in 2008. (Although Japan's GDP per labor input against the United States' level also hit the lowest point, around 17%, in 1948, it didn't fall too much.)

19 It is worth mentioning that, when we base our analysis on the cross-country data from the latest version of Penn World Table (PWT9.0) and Maddison, the economic growth rate we obtained is calculated using constant price in international currencies as benchmarks. We need to consider additionally the change of the renminbi exchange rate to convert the obtained growth rates into rates using constant price in renminbi as benchmark. We find no significantly positive or negative statistical correlation between exchange rate and development stages in all economies, including West European and East Asian economies. Moreover, like China, countries such as Japan and Korea have all undergone reforms that transform a fixed exchange rate system pegging the currency to dollar to a managed floating exchange rate system, and did not exit the currency peg smoothly. Therefore, for now we do not consider the change in renminbi to dollar exchange rate and its impact on the estimation of growth rate based on constant price in renminbi.

20 The two data sources are commonly used when scholars are observing long-term economic growth patterns and conducting cross-country comparisons.

21 China's 2008 GDP per labor input relative to that of the United States was around the same level with that of Japan in 1948, Taiwan in 1965, and Korea in 1968 (Singapore has never reached the same level as China's 2008 level). Our samples for projection are Japan (1948–), Taiwan (1965–), and Korea (1968–).

22 Here we briefly introduce the iteration process. We assume the annual growth rate of the United States' GDP per labor input equals the estimates of μ for future years as shown in Figures 1.1–1.7, respectively. For the first scenario, we can calculate China's growth rate of GDP per labor input in 2009 based on the data of both China and the United States' GDP per labor input in 2008 and thereby obtain China's GDP per labor input in 2009. Then we can obtain China's growth rate of GDP per labor input in 2010 based on the data of 2009 United States GDP per labor input. For the second scenario, for data based on GDP per labor

input in both countries in 2014 (data from Maddison (2010) and PWT9.0 end at 2008 and 2011, respectively), the discrepancy between the two countries' GDP data in overlapping years come mainly from the different amendments made to the GDP figures published by Chinese authorities (calculated in RMB) and the difference in purchasing power parity (PPP) exchange rates used for the conversion into constant international dollars. We have updated the data to 2014 based on the 2008 and 2014 China-US data ratio with data from PWT9.0 to obtain the growth rate of China's GDP per labor input in 2015, China's labor productivity in 2015, the United States' labor productivity in 2015, China's labor productivity in 2016, and so on and so forth.

23 The NBS data is the difference between real GDP growth rate (calculated with data of "GDP index (previous year=100)" from the NBS website) and labor force growth rate (calculated with data of "employment" from the NBS website) for each year.

24 NBS data in the figure "Total Population" is sourced from the NBS website and UN data come from *The World Population Prospects: 2015 Revision*; data in figure "Population Growth Rate" is calculated using "Total Population" data. *The World Population Prospects: 2015 Revision* gives low-, medium-, and high-fertility variant projections for Chinese population during 2015 to 2050. Considering the fact that the medium projection falls in the middle and age distribution for 2015 to 2050 is only provided under the medium projection (we will use the age distribution data in the following section), we choose this particular projection.

25 *The World Population Prospects: 2015 Revision* provides only the estimates of the population age structure for 2015 to 2100 in the "medium-fertility variant" scenario.

26 The employment participation rate is calculated based on the number of people employed and total population in PWT9.0.

27 Since China's dependency ratio has experienced upturn in 1970 and downturn in 2011 over the period 1950 to 2013, we only include the samples covering 1970 to 2011 in the quadratic form fitting. This has inherent economic logics: the higher the share of population aged 15–64, the higher the employment participation rate. However, an abundance of labor supply is more likely to be accompanied by redundancy, so when the share of population aged 15–64 rises, the employment participation rate will increase with a declining speed.

2 Is China's current slowdown a cyclical downturn or a long-run trend?

A productivity-based analysis

Introduction

Breathless reports that China had overtaken the United States as the world's largest economy since 2014 might be wrong (Frankel, 2016), while this in no respect detracts from China's impressive growth of about 10% per annum for three decades since 1978, which constitutes a historical miracle (Lin *et al.*, 1995; Prasad, 2009), and its visible signs of slowdown since the Global Financial Crisis (GFC for short hereafter) in 2008. According to its official statistics, the annual growth rate of China's real GDP dropped from 10.5% between 2000 and 2007 to 9.6% in 2008 and hit bottom at 9.2% in 2009. It then took a sharp turn downward in 2011 after a brief period of moderate recovery and touched a record low of 6.9% in 2015, the lowest since 1990. Many observers even suspect that the slowdown may have been greater and China's stimulus plan between 2009 and 2010 may induce distortions that sacrifice the long-term growth for its short-term stabilization target.

Whether this downshift is temporary (cyclical) or long lasting (structural) have been subject to much contention. Some blame the lower growth on transitory events such as the sluggishness of the recovery in advanced economies and the debt problems in Europe after the GFC (World Bank, 2014). They are optimistic that the Chinese economy will be back on its high-growth track, albeit at a somewhat slower pace, once the residual impact of the crises fades away (Lin, 2012). As China's per capita GDP is only about one-fourth of that for the United States, its institutional quality keeps improving, and its economy continues to integrate with the rest the world, these all imply a substantial growth potential in the foreseeable future. Moreover, as implied by the "flying geese" growth experience of Japan and the other East Asian tigers, China may prolong its rapid growth period as its less-developed provinces are continuing up the ladder following the path of their more-developed counterparts.

Others, however, argue that China's high-speed growth is unsustainable and thus predict a shift towards "lower gear" or a "New Normal" scenario in the foreseeable future. China's slowdown may be accelerated by its changing demographics and the accumulated structural issues underlying the development mode of the past decade. China starting out poor tends to conditionally grow faster, whereas it will begin to slow down when the gap with the leaders becomes narrow since technology catch-up by learning-by-doing and "easy" efficiency gains by reallocation become increasingly exhausted. Historically, countries on average exceed no more than 10 years of sustained rapid growth (Aizenman and Spiegel, 2010) and economies that once grew faster would sooner or later regress to the mean (Pritchett and Summers, 2014). China is now approaching or will soon approach the per capita income at which growth in many other countries began to decelerate (Eichengreen *et al.*, 2012, 2015).

A long list of potential reasons why rapidly growing countries in general and China in particular are expected to slow down can be made. Relevant discussions, however, have remained largely silent about quantitatively decomposing the causes of China's post-crisis slowdown. Obviously, China's post-crisis slowdown is caused by both cyclical and secular factors. The question is to what extent this slowdown reflects its structural bottlenecks that impede growth over the medium to long term. Moreover, as the three important conditions that facilitate China's fast growth in the past – unlimited labor supply, low-cost advantages, and rapid export expansion – all diminish steadily (Huang *et al.*, 2013; Frankel, 2016), and China's external environment is very likely to be less and less supportive to its growth, pursuing reforms and structural transformation that boost productivity is essentially needed. Both theory and evidence highlight the role of productivity in driving long-run growth, although there is not yet consensus on how to measure and estimate the decomposition of productivity.

Additionally, although China's cyclical downturn might be caused by short-term negative demand or supply shocks (or both), we argue the former is much less likely to be true since China watches labor costs soar while causing no serious unemployment. When an economy is facing demand shocks, its unemployment rate would escalate if prices were rigid; or, the wages would be unlikely to grow fast or even fall if prices could not adjust immediately. Therefore, we follow the growth accounting framework from the supply side to understand China's post-crisis downshift. According to our analysis (which will be discussed in details later), the annual productivity growth (growth rates of factor inputs subtracted) reached a rate of 3.55% between 1978 and 2007, much higher as compared to that of 1.97% over the period 2008 to 2014. Our analysis reveals that the economic slowdown since 2008 is a combined result of the decrease in both human capital and productivity growth rates. The cause of the former is readily explained by an increasingly aging population and more than two decades of widening coverage of compulsory education. A better understanding of what has led to the latter, therefore, is central to the accurate interpretation of the current slowdown in China's economic activity and the forecast of its performance in the future.

As such, this part first constructs provincial panel data of productivity growth between 1978 and 2014 based on the growth accounting model. In order to reveal potential factors of productivity growth, it examines three aspects, namely technical efficiency, the efficiency of factor utilization, and allocative efficiency. It then uses counter-factual analysis to decomposition the causes of variations in China's productivity growth in recent years and recursively simulate the effects of policy-promoted investment booms on economic growth.

The main novelty of this part is as follows. First, it offers a comprehensive estimate of China's national and provincial total factor productivity (TFP) over the period of 1978 to 2014 based on comparable data.[1] More specifically, it follows the principle of considering under-utilization of factors as an efficiency loss and differentiates between the amount of inputs and their production efficiency as much as possible when assessing the TFP. Second, it determines the impact of technical efficiency, the efficiency of factor utilization, and the allocative efficiency on the TFP with provincial panel data. The panel can help to simultaneously consider provincial and year fixed effects. The former is closely related to regional specific time-invariant characteristics over many years, whereas the latter reflects the cyclical effects on all provinces during the same period. Results from the panel can then be applied to reveal (long-run) effects of referred determinants on TFP when (short-run) cyclical shocks are controlled. Third, after assessing the annual level of labor resource in different provinces, the study adopts two methods to calculate the TFP: one considers human capital stock, which is a measure of quality-adjusted labor force, as labor input; the other takes only the working-age population into account but considers human capital as a determinant of the efficiency of factor utilization. Finally, it performs a counter-factual analysis to investigate the causes of China's post-crisis productivity variations in order to predict the long-term growth rate of the Chinese economy. It answers the question of whether China's economic slowdown since the 2008 financial crisis is a cyclical downturn or a long-run trend.

The rest of this part is summarized as follows. The first section summarizes a brief survey of the research on TFP, its estimation procedures, and the factors that determine its growth. The following section describes the analysis framework. Then, the next section explains the selection of indicators and data handling, and then applies the orthogonal decomposition method to identify effects of such indicators on productivity. The following sections describe how the authors break down the causes of the post-crisis fluctuation in productivity and recursively simulate the effects of policy-induced investment boom on growth using a counter-factual analysis. The final section concludes.

Literature review[2]

This section surveys two lines of literature: one on TFP and its estimation methods, the other on elements that have an impact on factor utilization.

1) TFP and estimation methods

The term total factor productivity (TFP) has its origin in a 1766 article by Quesnay, which mentioned the word "productivity" for the first time, referring to the output generated per unit of input. Its conceptual framework was later established in Tinbergen's international comparison in 1942. By linking the increase in output that cannot be explained by increase in input (Solow residual) to TFP, Solow (1957) set up the grounds for productivity measures in his neoclassical growth model. Abramovitz (1956) referred to the TFP as a "measure of our ignorance," pointing to the various sources of productivity growth that cannot be explained by the factor inputs. His work spawned a series of studies aiming to expand Solow's model, taking into account the measurement issue Abramovitz raised and trying to relate the resulted TFP to technological progress with commonly held beliefs.[3] However, Solow's TFP measures remain to date the most widely used methods in literature.

Domestic scholars started to take notice of China's TFP in the early 1980s. Shi *et al.* (1985) made some of the earliest attempts. Systematic application of growth accounting theories and methods to measure technological advancement in China, however, did not begin until the 1990s. Today, there is a large collection of studies on related topics. Generally speaking, the majority of them focus on providing estimates of TFP growth rate. Researches seeking to understand the change in TFP are relatively scarce.

Methodology is a central concern in obtaining TFP growth estimates. Theorists in this field are typically preoccupied with debating the merits of different production functions (i.e., which one more accurately describes the input-output production process) and uncovering their linkages. Empiricists, on the other hand, devote a large amount of effort to inferring the production process from input/output data. Several approaches are widely accepted in empirical studies, including Solow's (1957) growth accounting method, Farrell's (1957) deterministic production frontier, Aigner's (1977) stochastic production frontier, Charnes's (1978) data envelopment analysis, and Caves *et al.*'s (1982) Malmquist productivity index. All the available methods have pros and cons. However, the growth accounting method is perhaps the most appropriate for explaining the change in TFP (Barro and Sala-i-Martin, 1995; Barro, 1999).

Another issue of concern is how to measure factor input; more specifically, how to calculate the physical capital stock and whether to take human capital into account when considering labor input. Research studying China's TFP often centers on assessing the physical capital stock – most of such studies use the perpetual inventory method (PIM) (Goldsmith, 1951). Yet a major point of contention exists with respect to the assumptions of the initial physical capital stock and the depreciation rate (Ren and Liu, 1997). In addition, opinions are divided as to whether different types of capital should be first assessed separately and then added to the total physical capital stock (Bai *et al.*, 2006, 2007) or not (Zhang and Zhang, 2003; Zhang *et al.*, 2004; Perkins and Rawski, 2008).

One of the thorniest issues confronting scholars studying TFP is how to introduce human capital into the growth accounting model. It is indeed widely acknowledged that human capital accounts for impressive economic rise (Mankiw *et al.*, 1992). However, to date no consensus has emerged on the definition of human capital and subsequently, how to measure it. The work of Lu *et al.* (2004) is one of Chinese scholars' first forays into this field. An even more complex issue concerns the impact of human capital on growth. Scholars distinguish between the roles of human capital as a factor of production and a factor that affects the growth rate of TFP (Benhabib and Spiegel, 1994; Wei and Zhang, 2010), both through domestic innovations (Romer, 1990a) and by facilitating technological adoption and catchup (Nelson and Phelps, 1966). In the former, the benefit of human capital is measured as an input into the production process, whereas in the latter, its growth effects operate through the efficiency of input utilization.

2) *Factors affecting productivity rate*

The TFP, as Abramovitz cautioned, is not much more than "a measure of our ignorance" that to date has remained largely unexplained. Empirically speaking, the estimates of TFP are sensitive to the choice of method, researchers' selection of indicators to proxy the input-output process, and possible measurement errors in the original data. Although work devoted to the systematic decomposition of TFP growth is few and far between, scholars have looked at various areas in their attempt to explain the increase in TFP.

Many early studies sought to identify the source of TFP growth. For example, Arrow (1962) observed that productivity gains are achieved through learning-by-doing and spillovers. Romer (1990b), on the other hand, labeled firms' research and development (R&D) as a major source of growth in TFP. Other scholars further noted that increasing economic integration has facilitated technological spillovers through foreign direct investment (FDI) (MacDougall, 1960) and trade (Grossman and Helpman, 1991; He, 2007).

The allocation of production factors is of primary interest to scholars studying China's TFP. As Jones (2011) marked, income differences across countries associated with resource misallocation is one of the most important developments in the growth literature of the last decade. Scholars including Banerjee and Duflo (2005) and Restuccia and Rogerson (2008) have made attempts theoretically and empirically to prove the linkage between misallocation and the income gap between low-income countries and their industrialized peers. Many believe that reforms and policy adjustments aiming to correct resource misallocation in China have the capacity to unlock the country's huge growth potential (Hsieh and Klenow, 2009; Brandt *et al.*, 2012; Luo *et al.*, 2012).

Theoretical framework and analysis

This section offers first an explanation on how national and provincial TFP rates are estimated, followed by an introduction on ways of orthogonally decomposing TFP into several factors and an assessment of their marginal effects.

1) Methodologies for TFP estimation

Of the many TFP estimation methods, the growth accounting approach is well suited for exploring the factors influencing TFP. More specifically, this approach assumes a production function reflecting the relationship between the output Y, physical capital stock K, and human capital stock H, which takes the form of $Y = AK^{\alpha}H^{1-\alpha}$, where α is the capital income share and A the TFP. From the above production function we have $g_A = g_Y - \alpha g_K - (1-\alpha)g_H$, which implies that TFP growth rate (g_A) can be obtained once the growth rates of output (g_y), physical (g_k), and human capital stock (g_H), as well as the capital income share, are known.

We can rewrite the production function as $Y = A^{\frac{1}{1-\alpha}}\left(\dfrac{K}{Y}\right)^{\frac{\alpha}{1-\alpha}}H$ ($\dfrac{K}{Y}$ is the capital output ratio), from which we get $g_A = (1-\alpha)g_Y - \alpha g_{\frac{K}{Y}} - (1-\alpha)g_H$.

Thereby we can compute TFP growth rate for given measures of output growth rate, capital-output growth rate (g_K), human capital growth rate, and share of capital income. This study adopts the second approach since the neoclassical growth model implies a constant capital output ratio at steady state. This approach holds that the parallel growth in physical stock (accumulated by investment that is part of output) as that of output is assured by TFP (otherwise one would assume that decreasing marginal product would reduce investment and therefore lower accumulation of physical capital stock). In that sense, it would be better to attribute the growth in output resulting from such induced growth in physical capital to the TFP. The physical capital only further contributes to economic growth when it grows relatively faster than output, which means changes in capital output ratios or shifts of the growth path.

2) Determinants of TFP

TFP measures the portion of output not explained by the amount of inputs used in production. As such, the level of TFP (and by extension the efficiency of an economy's factor utilization) is determined by how efficiently and intensely the inputs are utilized in production (factors boosting efficient utilization of inputs) and how much output is generated per unit of input. In the latter, productivity gains can be attributed to technological progress and a range of other changes including economic, political, regulatory, and cultural developments. Regardless of the source, productivity growth is either reflected as a boost in overall productivity (technical efficiency) or an increase in average productivity when productivity enhancing reallocation incurs (allocative efficiency).[4]

We hence model TFP growth as a function of three groups of determinants including: 1) variables that will lead to improvement in the technical efficiency and, in turn, result in overall improvement in productivity (hereafter Group 1 determinants); 2) variables that will boost the efficient utilization of factors (Group 2 determinants); and 3) variables that will enhance efficient factor allocation (Group 3 determinants). The equation is expressed as follows:

$$tfp_{it} = \underbrace{\left(\phi_1 TE_{1,it} + \phi_2 TE_{2,it} + \cdots\right)}_{Group1 \ determinants} + \underbrace{\left(\varphi_1 EU_{1,it} + \varphi_2 EU_{2,it} + \cdots\right)}_{Group2 \ determinants} +$$

$$\underbrace{\left(\gamma_1 AE_{1,it} + \gamma_2 AE_{2,it} + \cdots\right)}_{Group3 \ determinants} + \Gamma X + \varepsilon_{it} \qquad (1)$$

Data source and indicators

This section first discusses how we estimate the annual provincial TFP and then explains our choice of indicators for the aforementioned three groups of determinants.

1) Provincial TFP

The first step in growth accounting exercises is to compute the capital income share, human capital stock, and output and physical capital stock in real terms using the most recently released data. The detailed procedure works as follows.

Annual real GRP by province (at 2005 constant price)

Data of provincial gross regional product (GRP for short) index from 1978 to 2014 (previous year = 100) is compiled from two sources: data over the 1978 to 1992 period is collected from the *China Compendium of Statistics over Sixty Years* and data for the period 1993 to 2014 is sourced from the website of China's National Bureau of Statistics (hereafter "NBS website" if no other specification of the data source is provided). Since the price base changes every year, these figures do not form a homogeneous time series. We therefore recalculate them in 2005 prices and then adjust them for inflation to obtain the provincial time series for real GRP at a 2005 constant price.[5]

Annual capital income share by province

Growth accounting literature (e.g., Chen *et al.*, 1988; Chow, 1993; Chou and Li, 2002) traditionally estimates the aggregate production function and from this derives the share of capital income. We find that this approach may be not applicable here for two reasons. First, such an approach produces a fixed share of capital income, which is empirically unlikely given that the time series we choose expands over 36 years. Second, empirical investigations of the aggregate production may be theoretically flawed, as they treat capital as an independent variable (because the change of capital is closely associated with the rate of return to capital, which in turn is largely affected by productivity). As Perkins and Rawski (2008) observed, "in China and other nations that experience major economic or institutional reforms, the growth of capital is itself in part the result of acceleration in TFP growth" (p6).

Here we compute the capital income share based on data of output structure accounted in income approach: data for 1978 to 1992 comes from *China Gross Domestic Product Estimates 1952–1995* and data for 1993 to 2014 comes from the NBS website. We exclude net production tax from the capital income share calculation because the taxable amount includes income from both capital and labor inputs,[6] expressed as follows:

$$\alpha_{it} = \frac{\text{depreciation on fixed assets}_{it} + \text{operating surplus}_{it}}{\text{compensation of employees}_{it} + \text{depreciation on fixed assets}_{it} + \text{operating surplus}_{it}}.$$

It is worth mentioning that the growth accounting method allows for the calculation of TFP only when the capital income share is fixed. It, however, may be far-fetched to claim a constant provincial annual share of capital income (e.g., using the average of the annual capital income shares as a proxy) over a very long horizon (1978 to 2014) of rapid transformation. Such an assumption ignores the change in income distribution within and across provinces over time. For this reason, we only assume that the current year's capital income share is the same as that of the previous year. In other words, we use the mean of the capital income share of year t and year $(t-1)$ to calculate year t's TFP growth rate for i province.

Annual human capital stock by province

The lack of a large-scale survey on the educational attainment of the population poses a challenge to directly measuring the provincial stock of human capital. In this part we opt to construct time series of stocks of educational attainment for the working-age population province by province. We begin with the time-series estimates of age-specific population structure and the average years of education attainment by age. Next we obtain the total years of education of the population in the working-age population (aged 15–64, following the United Nations standards) by taking a weighted sum of the average years of schooling received by each age group (weights are assigned to different age groups based on their size), which then is used as a proxy for human capital stock.[7] The details of this procedure are presented below.

Step 1: construct provincial population age structure. To date the Chinese government has conducted only six censuses and several population sampling surveys. Detailed age structures of provincial population of all these surveys is not disclosed to the public. Many demographic and sociological studies have made attempts to present an accurate portrait of national population age structure. There are, regrettably, far less similar endeavors made at the provincial level. We believe that the dynamics of provincial population change over time is well described by the Markov process, in which a given individual will either die (exit the economy) or move into the group aged one year older and, at the same time, a group aged 0 will be formed by newborns of that year. In the absence of interprovincial migration,[8] it is feasible to make inferences about historical and future patterns of provincial population age composition based on relevant data of a given year and every year's birth rate and age-specific mortality rates. Here we use the age-specific rates of mortality estimated by assuming $d_{a,i,t} = d_{i,t} \bullet \dfrac{d_{a,i,2000}}{d_{i,2000}}$ (where $d_{i,t}$ and $d_{a,i,t}$ is the mortality rate of the whole population and that of the population group aged *a* in province *i* in year *t*, respectively; $d_{i,2000}$ and $d_{a,i,2000}$ are the corresponding rates for the year 2000). The basic concept underlying the above assumption is that the possibility of death for any particular individual in a given year is affected both by their age and specific risk factors present in that year (reflected in that year's crude death rate).

Step 2: estimate provincial age-specific education attainment.[9] We first measure the average age-specific years of schooling received by the working-age population (15–64) based on individual data from the 2005 population census (the sample contains about 2.48 million people). Taking the population group aged 35 as an example, which is denoted by $Educyear35_{it}$, for any province *i* at any time *t*, we assign the number of average years of schooling for all individuals aged 35 from 2005 survey data as the realized value of $Educyear35_{it}$ in 2005, that for all individuals aged 36 as the realized value of $Educyear35_{it}$ in 2004,[10] that for all individuals aged 37 as the realized value of $Educyear35_{it}$ in 2003,[11] and so forth. Similarly, we get realized values of $Educyear35_{it}$ between years 2006 and 2014 from the 2010 census data. For all other age groups between 15 and 64 of each province, we estimate their average years of schooling in a similar way.[12]

Annual physical capital stock by province

Following Bai *et al.* (2006, 2007), we use the PIM to measure the annual provincial physical capital stock. We first compute the annual provincial physical capital stock (at 2005 constant price) for construction and installation and that for equipment separately, and then add them up to obtain the aggregate annual provincial physical capital stock.[13]

Figure 2.1 shows the distribution of the provincial TFP growth rates from 1978 to 2014 (frequencies are shown on the left vertical axis, the corresponding fitted kernel density shown on the right vertical axis). Results when human capital is included (with human capital stock as an input, tfp_{hc}) and excluded (with the working-age population in the 15–64 cohorts as an input, tfp_{wp}) are both displayed in the figure.[14] The growth rates of TFP (written as $\{tfp_{it}\}$, which reflects the change in overall productivity) obtained with or without a human capital variable is quite similar. As such, we start with tfp_{hc} and use tfp_{wp} (where human capital is additionally considered as a utilization-efficiency determinant) as a robustness check in the following analysis.

2) Factors of changes in productivity

As mentioned previously, the "residual" TFP measures the portion of output not explained by the amount of tangible, and therefore quantifiable, inputs

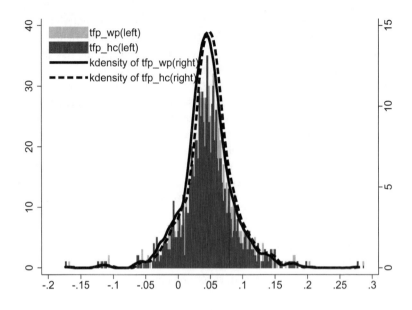

Figure 2.1 Distribution of the average TFP growth rate from 1978 to 2014

used in production. As such, the growth of TFP can be attributed either to a rise in aggregate productivity (potential productivity), or an increase in input utilization rate, or more efficient allocation of factor input between different production sectors. In this part, we denote the three groups of determinants as "technical efficiency," "utilization efficiency," and "allocative efficiency," respectively.

Specifically, Group 1 determinants (technical efficiency) act on the utilization of capital and/or labor inputs in different sectors simultaneously. Institutional quality (e.g., rule of law), technological progress (neutral, labor-augmenting, and capital-augmenting), and openness to the world economy are some well-studied examples. Economic catch-up (or convergence) as reflected in income levels relative to the world frontier also falls under this category.

We introduce Group 2 determinants (utilization efficiency) for the following two reasons. First, although it is the flow of services from the capital stock and the people employed that make active contribution to the output, under-utilization of available capital and labor resource is in itself a loss of efficiency, which therefore should be captured by the estimated TFP. Hence, to fully separate the effects of the amount and the utilization efficiency of inputs, we recommend to estimate TFP by considering all physical capital stock (whether used or not) and the entire working-age population (whether employed or not) as production inputs. Second, given that the demand-side factors mainly influence the short-term utilization efficiency of inputs whereas the supply-side factors mainly affect the amount of available resource in the long run, it is only natural that we seek to separate the effects of the latter from the former.

Group 3 determinants (allocative efficiency) are well explored in the misallocation literature. Resource reallocation often affects factor utilization, given the productivity gap between, for example, government and households, state-owned enterprises (SOEs) and non-SOE firms, urban and rural areas, different industries, and investment goods and consumer goods sectors.[15] As the "reform dividends" literature (among other research) observed, sectoral reallocation has been a major source of economic growth since China's reforms and opening up. Therefore, even when sector-specific productivity remained constant, structural reforms could enhance overall productivity by changing the relative weight of different sectors in the economy. By choosing appropriate indicators such as government size, the share of state ownership, urbanization progress, and the weights of the primary and the tertiary sectors in the economy, it is possible to measure the effects of resource reallocation resulting from structural reforms.

We identify two major indicators associated with Group 1 determinants: 1) provincial income level (the catch-up indicator, or the CUI for short), which measures the catch-up effect, defined as the natural logarithm of relative provincial lagged real GRP per capita to lagged real GDP per capita of the United States (written as *L.*ln*relativeGRP*);[16] and 2) the degree of dependence on foreign trade, which reflects the level of openness and trade orientation of a provincial economy and its capacity to capture technology spillovers, defined as the ratio of exports and imports to GRP (written as *ftd*). Imports and exports data used to calculate this indicator are expressed in US dollars (data for the period 1978 to 1992 is sourced from *The Compendium of Statistical Data and Materials on 50 Years of New China*, data for 1993 to 2014 is sourced from the NBS website)[17] and thus needs to be converted into RMB. We make this conversion by first obtaining the annual USD/CNY bid and ask rates based on national layer data (the NBS website provides annual data on total imports and exports both in USD and RMB).[18]

Group 2 determinants include variables that affect the level of output generated per unit of input through effective usage. We select two indicators. The first indicator is the provincial inventory stock, which measures the accumulation of non-productive capital, defined as the ratio of inventory stock to GRP (written as *inventory*). We adopt an approach similar to the one used to calculate the physical capital stock to assess the real inventory stock (in 2005 prices). Data needed in calculation is gathered from the NBS website and the *China Compendium of Statistics 1949–2008*. The second indicator is the employment participation rate, which measures the proportion of the working-age population active in the production process, defined as the percentage of employed persons in population aged 15–64 (written as *epr*).

This indicator can be derived from multiplying the proportion of economically active persons (or labor force) in the working-age population (the labor participation rate, or LPR for short, as it is commonly called) with that of employed persons in the labor force (the so-called employment rate). In our opinion, the former mainly reflects the health status and working willingness of the Chinese working-age population, whereas the latter mainly indicates how active they are in the economy; their products, here termed as the employment participation rate, therefore show comprehensively the efficiency of potential labor input (all working-age population) to actual labor input (employment). Data on the total number of employed persons comes mainly from the *China Compendium of Statistics 1949–2008*, complemented by information from provincial statistical yearbooks, statistical bulletins of human resources and social security development, and statistical bulletins of national economic and social development. The detailed estimation of the working-age population (15–64) can be found above.

We only introduce human capital intensity *princomp_hc* as a third indicator when tfp_{wp} is used as a dependent variable. Human capital intensity as a composition factor is defined as the weighted average of age-specific education attainments of the working-age population (15–64), which can be calculated using the Principal Component Analysis (PCA) method. Specifically, we use the principal component as a proxy for human capital intensity.

The indicators for the Group 3 determinants include government size, the weight of SOEs in the economy, investment rate, industrial structure, urbanization, and migration. Government size and the weight of SOEs in the economy are two variables that measure the influence of government intervention on TFP growth. Investment rate measures the factor utilization difference between investment goods sectors and consumer goods sectors. Industrial structure measures the productivity gap between different economic sectors. Urbanization and migration measures the effects of factor mobility.

Government size is defined as the ratio of local government revenue to provincial GRP (written as *govsize*).[19] Annual local government revenue data (in current prices) is collected from the NBS website (local government budgets and expenditures sector).[20] Provincial GRP (in current prices) data for the period 1993 to 2014 comes from the NBS website; that for the period 1978 to 1992 comes from *China Compendium of Statistics 1949–2008*.

The economic weight of SOEs (written as *soe*) is defined as the ratio of investment in fixed asset by state-owned enterprises (SOEs) to the aggregate investment in fixed asset.[21] Data for the period 1978 to 2004 is sourced from *China Compendium of Statistics 1949–2004*; that for the period 2005 to 2014 comes from the NBS website.

Investment rate (written as *inv_rate*) is defined as the ratio of aggregate capital formation to provincial GRP. Data for the period 1993 to 2014 comes from the NBS website; that for the period 1978 to 1992 comes from the *China Compendium of Statistics 1949–2008*.

Industrial structure includes the weight of the primary sector (written as *prim*) and the weight of the third sector (written as *third*). The former is defined as the share of the value added of the primary sector in provincial GRP. The latter is defined as the share of the value added of the third sector in provincial GRP. Data for the period 1993 to 2014 comes from the NBS website; that for the period 1978 to 1992 comes from the *China Compendium of Statistics 1949–2008*.

Urbanization is defined as the growth rate of the share of urban population in total population (written as *urgr*). Data of the share of urban population for the period 2000 to 2014 is from the NBS website; data for the period 1978 to 1999 is collected from *The China Compendium of Statistics 1949–2008*.

Migration includes the rate of entrance (written as *migratein*) and the rate of exit (written as *migrateout*),[22] both of which measure the effect of interregional labor mobility on TFP growth. The introduction of this indicator could at least partially correct the bias of assuming the lack of migration among provinces previously when calculating provincial human capital stock. Data of these two indicators between 1978 and 2010 comes from several sources: that for the period 1978 to 1984 is from *The Demographic Data Assembly of the People's Republic of China 1949–1985*; that for years between 1985 and 1991 is correspondingly collected from various of *Almanac of China's Population Statistics* for years between 1986 and 1991; that for years from 1992 to 2010 is accordingly from various issues of *County Level of Population Statistics in the People's Republic of China* for years from 1992 to 2010.

Table 2.1 presents the summary statistics for all aforementioned variables.

Table 2.1 Summary statistics and unit root tests for key variables

		Obs.	*Mean*	*Std.*	*Min.*	*Max.*
TFP growth	tfp_hc	1106	0.046	0.037	−0.181	0.270
rate	tfp_wp	1106	0.050	0.037	−0.176	0.279
L.InrelativeGRP		1147	−3.461	0.570	−4.686	−1.757
Ftd		1109	0.228	0.337	0.001	1.912

(*Continued*)

Table 2.1 (Continued)

	Obs.	Mean	Std.	Min.	Max.
inventory	1147	0.650	0.331	0.072	2.740
Epr	1144	0.746	0.093	0.373	0.981
princomp_hc	1147	−0.033	6.212	−21.251	21.693
govsize	1136	0.104	0.065	0.006	0.620
Soe	1137	0.581	0.227	0.114	1.000
inv_rate	1140	0.453	0.151	0.138	1.304
Prim	1147	0.219	0.126	0.005	0.606
Third	1147	0.341	0.098	0.087	0.779
Urgr	1138	0.033	0.090	−0.652	0.903
migratein (‰)	993	17.907	7.165	1.980	61.250
migrateout (‰)	963	15.812	6.847	2.720	66.020

3) Determinants' effects on TFP growth

Given that Hausman test confirms fixed-effect models to be better than random-effect ones, we further use fixed-effect models to orthogonally decompose effects of the above potential determinants on TFP growth rate in the following analysis.

We also test the stationarity of residuals in the fixed-effect regression to ensure that the estimates are reliable and cointegration relationship exists between the TFP growth rate and the potential determinants.[23] On the basis of the tests suggested by Wooldridge (2003), we find that the fixed-effect regression continues to suffer from autocorrelation problems. We therefore report Newey-West standard deviations.

The tfp_{hc} approach

The first part (Columns 1 to 4) of Table 2.2 presents the results when we adopt the tfp_{hc} approach, namely estimating TFP growth rate when human capital is treated as a quality multiplier to adjust labor force.

Column 1 includes all potential variables of the above three groups of determinants. It finds that technical efficiency-related indicators – namely, income level ($L.lnrelativeGRP$) and degree of foreign trade dependence (ftd) – both have statistically significant impact on TFP growth rate. The estimated coefficient on the former variable has the expected negative sign, as convergence to the productivity frontier naturally entails a slowdown of TFP growth in the larger economy. The coefficient on the latter variable has the expected positive sign, confirming the common belief that learning and adaptation of advanced technology facilitated by a high level of openness raise productivity.

The utilization-efficiency indicators, the relative size of inventory stock (*inventory*), is found to have an expected negative impact on tfp_{hc}; whereas employment participation rate (*epr*) is found to have an expected, significantly positive effect on tfp_{hc}. Indeed, an increase in inventory stock implies a decrease in the amount of output entering the production process, whereas a higher employment participation rate means more working-age people entering the work force.

Allocative-efficiency indicators such as government size (*govsize*) have a significant negative effect, as expected, whereas the economic weight of SOEs (*soe*) appears to have an insignificant effect. Slightly inconsistent with commonly held belief, results shown in Column 1 suggest that state ownership may not necessarily reduce efficiency. One possible explanation is the choice of indicator. We proxy the weight of SOEs in the investment in fixed assets to that in the whole economy. Moreover, the insignificance of the corresponding efficiency may be a result of two opposing effects. As Bai *et al.* (2000) observed, SOEs have positive spillover effects. Such positive impacts on the economy could be offset by the well-documented negative impacts associated with monopoly and resource under-utilization. The observed insignificance may also be a result of the synchronous relationship influenced by a third factor (i.e., economic prosperity): an expansion of the state-owned economy and growth in productivity would be simultaneously observed during the economic boom.

Results of investment rate (*inv_rate*) along with its square terms to show possible non-linear effects indicate insignificant inverted U-shape effect of this indicator on tfp_{hc}. The estimated coefficients for industrial structure (*prim* and *third*), migration (*migratein* and *migrateout*), and urbanization (*urgr*) turn out to be statistically insignificant.

The statistically insignificant estimate of the square term of investment rate (*inv_rate*) then suggests the omission of this variable in Column 2. Moreover, given the missing migration data (*migratein* and *migrateout*) for certain years (mainly since 2011) and the imperfect representation for the economic weight of SOEs (*soe*), together with the insignificant impact of these three indicators (their estimated coefficients are close to zero and are statistically insignificant), we recalculate the estimates when excluding these indicators. The results are shown in Column 3. Clearly, the estimated coefficients in Columns 2 to 3 are close to their counterparts in Column 1, except for statistically significant estimates for the variable *inv_rate*.

For an economy undergoing dramatic transformation, China may have experienced significant structural changes within the time horizon under

Table 2.2 Determinants of TFP growth rate

	tfp_{hc}				tfp_{wp}		
	1978–2014		2001–2014		1978–2014		2001–2014
	(1)	(2)	(3)	(4)	(5)	(6)	(7)
L.lnrelativeGRP	-0.075***	-0.075***	-0.066***	-0.065**	-0.097***	-0.080***	-0.067**
	(0.013)	(0.013)	(0.011)	(0.028)	(0.015)	(0.012)	(0.028)
ftd	0.028***	0.028***	0.027***	0.007	0.026***	0.026***	0.007
	(0.009)	(0.009)	(0.008)	(0.013)	(0.009)	(0.008)	(0.013)
inventory	-0.020**	-0.020**	-0.012	0.000	-0.023**	-0.011	-0.003
	(0.009)	(0.009)	(0.008)	(0.020)	(0.010)	(0.008)	(0.020)
epr	0.081***	0.081***	0.074***	0.063	0.083***	0.071***	0.053
	(0.028)	(0.027)	(0.023)	(0.039)	(0.028)	(0.023)	(0.040)
princomp_hc					0.008***	0.005***	0.006
					(0.002)	(0.002)	(0.004)
govsize	-0.108**	-0.108**	-0.113***	-0.083	-0.108**	-0.102**	-0.084
	(0.046)	(0.045)	(0.041)	(0.162)	(0.046)	(0.041)	(0.149)
soe	0.002	0.002			-0.000		
	(0.014)	(0.014)			(0.014)		
inv_rate	-0.052	-0.052**	-0.049***	-0.068***	-0.100	-0.031*	-0.053***
	(0.073)	(0.023)	(0.016)	(0.014)	(0.072)	(0.018)	(0.017)
inv_rate square	-0.000				0.060		
	(0.060)				(0.063)		
prim	0.009	0.009	-0.029	-0.393***	0.027	-0.010	-0.363***
	(0.045)	(0.045)	(0.039)	(0.098)	(0.046)	(0.040)	(0.104)
third	-0.039	-0.039	-0.055	-0.109**	-0.055	-0.071*	-0.128**
	(0.041)	(0.041)	(0.033)	(0.045)	(0.044)	(0.037)	(0.054)
urgr	0.012	0.012	0.014	0.009	0.009	0.012	0.010

	(1)	(2)	(3)	(4)	(5)	(6)
migratein	0.000			0.000		
	(0.011)	(0.010)	(0.016)	(0.010)	(0.010)	(0.017)
	(0.000)			(0.000)		
migrateout	−0.000			−0.000		
	(0.001)			(0.001)		
Province effects	Yes	Yes	Yes	Yes	Yes	Yes
Year effects	Yes	Yes	Yes	Yes	Yes	Yes
Observations	939	1,095	432	939	1,095	432
IPS test	0.000	0.000	0.000	0.000	0.000	0.000

Notes: 1) The Newey-West standard deviations are in parentheses. 2) *, ** and *** denote significance at the 10%, 5% and 1% levels, respectively. 3) For the Im-Pesaran-Shin (IPS) test, we report the P-values.

investigation (1978 to 2014). In other words, a certain determinant's effect on. tfp_{hc}. may vary over time. An illustrative example is how "investment" could play a different role in different development stages: in early stages, investment (in particular investment on infrastructure) served to promote resource reallocation and productivity growth; it, however, could prove to be detrimental in later stages when over-investment leads to investment/consumption imbalance. Hence in Column 4 we focus on the 2001 to 2014 time period, which can be conveniently divided into two intervals of the same length before and after the 2008 crisis. We find similar values for the estimated coefficients. Under this approach, however, the degree of foreign trade dependence (*ftd*), relative size of inventory stock (*inventory*), employment participation rate (*epr*), and government size (*govsize*) have insignificant impact on tfp_{hc}; whereas the two indicators for industrial structure (*prim* and *third*) both have significantly negative impact.[24]

The tfp_{wp} approach

As previously discussed, human capital can be both viewed as a factor and a determinant of the efficiency of factor utilization. Results obtained using the first approach are displayed in the first part of Table 2.2 (Columns 1 to 4). The following section discusses results obtained when adopting the second approach. In other words, tfp_{wp} is turned into an explained variable and human capital intensity (*princomp_hc*) is entered as utilization-efficiency variable. Results are shown in the second part of Table 2.2 (Columns 5 to 7).

Clearly, human capital intensity (*princomp_hc*) has a significant, positive impact on TFP growth rate (tfp_{wp}). In addition, although the effects of individual indicators on the TFP growth rates in part 1 and part 2 are similar, they are, however, more pronounced in the former. We use regressions to orthogonally decompose effects of potential determinants on productivity because TFP as "a measure of our ignorance" to date has remained largely unexplained. Further, data limitation prevents us from directly revealing influences of these determinants. The human capital, however, can be more or less estimated (as we have done in earlier sections). We therefore adopt the tfp_{hc} approach to decompose the causes of China's post-crisis slowdown of productivity growth in the next section.

Decomposing the recent decline in productivity growth

In this section, we analyze the difference in TFP growth rate between two time intervals – 2001 to 2007 and 2008 to 2014 – and then determine the extent to which the gap could be explained by the change in individual determinants before and after 2008 (see Table 2.3).

To be more specific, we first calculate the TFP growth rate (in the tfp_{hc} situation with human capital included) and the values for the four indicators – relative income level ($L.\ln relativeGDP$),[25] investment rate (inv_rate), and industrial structure ($prim$ and $third$) – year by year over the period of 2001 to 2014 at the national level.[26] Then we compare the mean values of these four indicators before and after 2008. Based on a given determinant's average effect on TFP growth (which is obtained applying the estimated coefficient from Column 4 in Table 2.2), we next compute percentage of change in TFP growth rate after 2008 that can be explained by the change in a given determinant. As Table 2.3 clearly shows, China suffered a drop (0.019) in TFP growth rate after 2008, about 95.08% of which could be attributed to the four growth determinants.

In order to further explore the causes of China's post-crisis productivity variations, we adopt a counter-factual analysis (CFA) approach under a comparative static situation. In other words, in order to assess the growth effects attributable to a candidate determinant, we assume that only this particular determinant remains constant during the observing period and look at the "outcome" in the absence of its "intervention." The impact the determinant has on TFP growth rate (i.e., the explainable percentage) is then estimated by comparing CFA predictions to actual observations. Letting the candidate determinant be x, the CFA predictions are given by the equation $tfp_{\text{no }x,t}^{CFA} = tfp_t - \hat{\beta}_x \bullet (x_t - x_0)$ where tfp_t refers to the actual outcomes, $\hat{\beta}_x$ is the estimated marginal impact of x on productivity (which equals the estimated coefficient of x in Column 4 of Table 2.2), and x_0 and x_t stand for the original value of x and the value of x in a given year during the observing period, respectively. The "comparative static" analysis is so called to be distinguished from the later dynamic analysis, as this approach neglects the interactive effects among these determinants over years.[27]

Before proceeding further, it is useful to look at the combined effect of the four indicators on the TFP growth rate during 2008 to 2014. Figure 2.2 is a graphic demonstration of this effect (the "without time trend" curve), calculated based on estimated coefficients from Column 4 in Table 2.2 and values for the four indicators from 2008 to 2014, and its prediction when cyclical effects (namely the estimated time dummies from Column 4 in Table 2.2) are included (the "with time trend" curve).[28]

Figure 2.2 shows that the "with time trend" curve co-moves closely with the trend of data between 2008 and 2014, when both long-run trend (as predicted by the four indicators) and short-run cyclical variations (as implied by estimated time dummies) are considered. This further lends support to

Table 2.3 Change in TFP growth rate before and after 2008 and the percentage explainable by growth determinants

	Interval mean		Change after 2008		Percentage explained (%)
	2001–2007	2008–2014	Change	Marginal effect of change on TFP	
tfp$_{hc}$	0.0388	0.0197	−0.0191		−
L.lnrelativeGDP	−3.2787	−2.9693	0.3094	−0.0201	105.43
inv_rate	0.3986	0.4665	0.0678	−0.0046	24.14
prim	0.1224	0.0964	−0.0260	0.0102	−53.52
third	0.4188	0.4520	0.0332	−0.0036	19.03
Total	−	−	−	−0.0181	95.08

Notes: 1) All items presented in this table are authors' estimates (for methods of calculation and data source, see previous discussion). 2) Percentage explainable by a given determinant is given by the following equation: explainable percentage = change in determinant after 2008 * estimated coefficient / change in TFP growth rate after 2008 (*tfp$_{hc}$*).

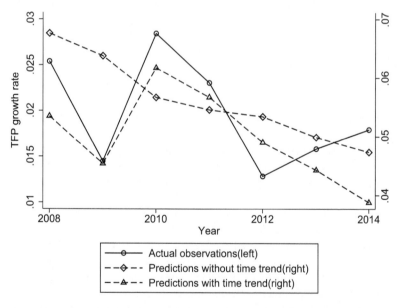

Figure 2.2 Change in TFP growth rate and its source from 2008 to 2014

the validity of orthogonally decomposing effects of potential determinants with panel data, as we have done in previous sections. The "without time trend" curve indicates that it is the long-run structural factors (when only the

---

four determinants are included) that are mainly responsible for the decrease in TFP growth rate during this period, rather than short-run cyclical factors. The differences between the "with" and "without time trend" curves result from influences of policies (excluding investment stimulus) and many other factors during this period.

Table 2.4 presents the CFA estimates of the growth effects of four indicators for the period 2008 to 2014. The figures in the first part of CFA estimates show what the CFA productivity growth rate would be over the period 2008 to 2014 and how it would change if we fix a certain candidate determinant from 2008 onwards at the 2007 level while allowing all the others to take their actual values. The differences between the corresponding CFA estimates and the actual observations (as shown in the last row) can be treated as the marginal effects of the particular determinant on productivity growth.

In summary, the continued faster growth of the Chinese economy relative to the United States' since the financial crisis has slowed down the convergence process. The changes in investment rate and the weight of the tertiary industry have combined to impede the continued improvement in TFP growth. Their negative influence has far outweighed the positive impact brought by the decrease in the weight of the primary industry. Should all four indicators remain constant at the 2007 level, the growth rate of China's productivity would have risen by 0.006, 0.009, 0.016, 0.018, 0.020, 0.023, and 0.026 in 2008, 2009, 2010, 2011, 2012, 2013, and 2014, respectively. Of all the three factors acting against growth in productivity, diminishing late-mover advantage as implied by higher relative income level is the primary culprit of this slowdown, followed by investment rate and the weight of the tertiary industry.

Given that the Chinese economy is set on an upward track, with relative higher growth rate than that of the United States for years to come, the investment rate is likely to remain high and the tertiary industry will keep expanding in the short term. Consequently, the slowdown since 2008

Table 2.4 CFA predictions of TFP determinants from 2008 to 2014

		2008	2009	2010	2011	2012	2013	2014
CFA predictions	L.lnrelativeGDP	0.030	0.021	0.042	0.039	0.029	0.034	0.039
	inv_rate	0.027	0.018	0.033	0.028	0.017	0.020	0.022
	Prim	0.025	0.013	0.026	0.020	0.010	0.012	0.013
	Third	0.025	0.016	0.030	0.025	0.016	0.020	0.024
Actual observations		0.025	0.014	0.028	0.023	0.013	0.016	0.018

Notes: 1) The "actual observations" in the above table are the national TFP growth rates (tfp_{hc}) for 2008–2014. 2) "CFA predictions" are estimates calculated holding a given determinant constant at the 2007 level. The difference between CFA predictions and their corresponding actual observations reflects the marginal effect of this particular determinant on the growth rate of productivity.

will become an inevitable trend for the conceivable future. The need to find new ways to raise productivity is urgent and real. Policies to facilitate trade openness and the optimal allocation of resources, as well as to support full employment, are a good start to improving China's productivity and, subsequently, economic growth in the long term.

Roles of the stimulus policy-induced investment surge

The massive stimulus package rolled out by the government in the wake of the 2008 financial crisis has had a discernable effect: the Chinese economy has been able to continue to expand at a relatively fast pace in spite of the tumbling productivity growth. Our concern is with the role the package and, in particular, the surge in investment induced by the package played in this process. In this section, we adopt the counter-factual analysis (specifically, the dynamic approach) to investigate how the interaction between investment rate (*inv_rate*) and other determinants affect TFP growth.

First, again (see previous section) we maintain investment rate on construction, installation, and equipment at the 2007 level whereas all other determinants take actual, observed values. We then calculate TFP growth rates and physical capital stock for 2008 based on the estimated coefficients in Column 4 in Table 2.2. The GDP for 2008 is obtained next by substituting relevant estimates into the equation $\dot{Y} = \frac{1}{1-\alpha}\dot{A} + \frac{\alpha}{1-\alpha}\left(\dot{K}/Y\right) + \dot{H}^{29}$, with which we are able to assess the TFP growth rate for 2009 based on an assumed investment rate for the same year. The same procedures are then repeated to compute the physical capital stock and the GDP for 2009, and so forth. Combined with CFA predictions, we obtain the growth rates of the national economy, capital output ratio, and TFP growth rates. Further, we hold the ratio of aggregate capital formation to GDP (i.e., investment rate) fixed at the 2007 level while allowing the share of government spending in GDP and share of net exports in GDP to take observed values.[30] Based on this estimated GDP data, we compute consumption and, thereupon, its growth rate for 2008 to 2014.

Figure 2.3 consists of four charts that compare, respectively, the growth rates of the economy, TFP, capital output ratio, and consumption with those predicted by CFA. Several observations from Figure 2.3 can be made. First, the rise in investment rate has effectively mitigated the negative impact of the financial crisis on the growth of the Chinese economy; its effect is most evident for 2009 and 2010. If China could have maintained its investment rate at the 2007 level (41.24%) over the consecutive years, its annual economic growth rate would have dropped to 9.64%, 8.03%, 9.37%, 8.62%, 7.08%, 7.09%, and 7.01%, below the actual observations by 0.06, 1.37,

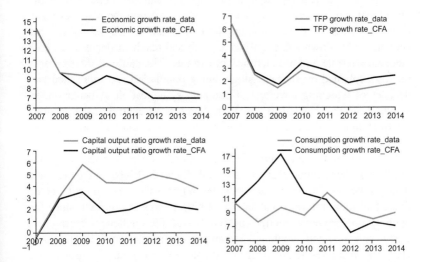

Figure 2.3 Impact of investment surge over the period 2008 to 2014

1.23, 0.88, 0.82, 0.71, and 0.29 percentages, respectively. Second, increasing investment rate has a negative effect on the TFP growth rate in the same duration (cutting the TFP growth rates by 0.13, 0.33, 0.52, 0.61, 0.61, 0.66, and 0.67 percentages, respectively). Its effect on the capital input is the opposite (the capital output ratio has ascended by 0.31, 2.41, 2.56, 2.30, 2.23, 2.27, and 1.88 percentages, respectively). Investment rate's impact on consumption, however, is less consistent. From 2008 to 2010, the increase in investment drove the growth rate of consumption down by 5.83, 7.48, and 3.12 percentages, respectively, whereas the former's continued rise since 2011 was emulated by the latter (consumption's growth rate increased by 0.94, 3.05, 0.58, and 1.96 percentages, respectively).

All in all, the investment rate experienced a sharp climb and remained at a high plateau between 2008 and 2014. Although it has, generally speaking, alleviated the negative effects of the financial crisis, it does so by harming the productivity improvement and impeding the consumption growth. Moreover, it failed to put the brakes on the long-term slowdown of China's economy.

Conclusion

The causes of China's slowdown in the aftermath of the 2008 financial crisis and its economic outlook have been subject to much contention. The answers have particularly important policy implications. Some believe that this slowdown is merely a cyclical downturn that may be soon reversed. Others consider it the start of a long-term structural trend. We find that the economic slowdown since 2008 is a combined result of decrease in both labor growth rate and productivity growth rate. The cause of the former is readily explained by an increasingly aging population and more than two decades of widening coverage of compulsory education. A better understanding of what has led to the latter, therefore, is central to the accurate interpretation of the current slowdown in China's economic activity and forecast of its performance in the future.

Existing literature on China's TFP has applied a variety of methods to survey TFP at the sectoral, regional, and national levels based on the available data. Studies sought out to trace different sources of TFP movement include those that link "reform dividends" to China's economic growth since the opening up. However, model uncertainty and the challenges researchers face in selecting and handling data hamper a consensus on TFP estimation. Building on studies that investigate the source of potential TFP growth, we first select a series of robust indicators, construct comparable time series from historical records, and then estimate the provincial and national TFP. Next we examine three aspects (namely technical efficiency, utilization efficiency, and allocative efficiency) to explain the evolving pattern of China's productivity growth based on the orthogonal decomposition method using panel data, which allows us to control both regional and year fixed effects. Finally, we apply counter-factual analysis to decompose the national factor utilization movement from 2008 onwards and simulate the effectiveness of the stimulus-induced investment surge as a tool in mitigating the impact of the financial crisis.

The results suggest that, first, in terms of technical efficiency, economic openness and relative income level both have an expected significant impact on productivity, although the former has a positive effect and the latter has a negative effect. Second, a significantly negative correlation is observed between inventory stock and productivity through its influence on effective factor usage; the opposite is observed between employment participation rate and productivity. As for indicators acting on factor utilization, government size and investment rate both have significantly negative effects on productivity; weights of the primary and the tertiary industries tend to be negatively correlated with productivity growth. State ownership and population migration, however, depict no statistically significant effects. Lastly, a decrease in late-mover advantage and growth in investment rate are both major contributors to the recent decline in China's productivity growth since the financial crisis. Moreover, although the stimulus-induced rise in investment has effectively mitigated the negative effects of the financial crisis on China's growth, it is not conducive to the growth of productivity and consumption. Therefore, we believe that the Chinese economy will continue to slow down in the foreseeable future. Policies to facilitate trade openness and the optimal allocation of resources, and support full employment are a good start to improve China's productivity and, subsequently, economic growth in the long-term.

This study is certainly not devoid of flaws. For example, we still rely on historical data. We choose to ignore the nuanced effect of migration when we estimate human capital stock and working-age population. Moreover, we consider a suboptimal method of econometric regression analysis to identify determinants of productivity; the regression results we obtained are better suited to describe the correlation (instead of casualty) between TFP growth rate and the indicators we choose. In addition, our counter-factual analysis conveniently ignores the effect the interaction between determinants (except the investment rate) could have on TFP growth rate. The issues outlined above could all be interesting directions for future research.

Notes

1 China's provincial level administrative units consist of provinces, municipalities, and autonomous regions, all addressed as "province" in this study for simplicity.
2 Detailed discussion of this section can be found in Bai and Zhang (2014).
3 Included among these studies are Denison (1967, 1972), Jorgenson and Griliches (1967), Christensen and Jorgenson (1969, 1970), etc.
4 For example, factors flow from less to more productive sectors or, in extreme cases, the least productive sectors are weeded out.
5 Principally speaking, so long as a single, fixed base year is chosen, price variation across provinces will have little effect on the final results. However, given the continuous adjustment made to the official data, the effect of provincial TFP determinants may not be accurately measured if we use time series expressed in prices of the previous year. As such, we pick 2005 as the fixed benchmark year, as opposed to the typical choice of 1952 or 1978, although our robustness analysis shows that choosing a different reference year (such as 1978) has no significant impact on the results.
6 This is a simplified assumption when detailed data on the tax burden of capital as well as labor are not available.
7 An alternative case of considering working-age population as those aged 20–60 delivers very similar results, which are not reported for space limitation but are available upon request.
8 This assumption can be readily accepted when estimating population structures at the national level since the amount of emigrants and immigrants are negligible when compared with China's domestic population. However, it may not be feasible to apply such an assumption at the provincial level. Still we make

such simplified assumptions for two reasons. One is that detailed annual data on age-specific migrants (or more specifically, age-specific migrants by education levels) is not publicly available. The other is that, migration (reallocation of population) itself may influence utilization efficiency of factors and therefore should be included as a determinant of productivity. Consequently, here we make this assumption when estimating human capital stock, while adding variables of migration as determinants of productivity later.

9 We assume an education system where an individual "starts school at six years old, receives six years of primary and three years of secondary education, three years of high school, two years of junior college or four years of undergraduate, and then two years of graduate education." Also, graduates from a certain educational level obtain all years of that level, while dropouts and those who have completed the schooling without earning a diploma or alternative credential of that level obtain half of the years (or, equivalently, assuming uniform distribution of dropout for that education level). Since school students are not classified as an economically active population, they are excluded from the following calculating process. We exclude them in the following way: taking individuals aged 20 with high school education when surveyed in 2005 (they are born in 1985), they should be students between 1991 and 2003, and thus we exclude them when calculating average education attainment for years before 2003.

10 Individuals aged 35 in 2004 form the group aged 36 in 2005 if they live on for another year; in this sense, the group aged 36 in 2005 is the best representative of the group aged 35 in 2004.

11 Individuals aged 35 in 2003 become 37 in 2005 if they survive.

12 Note that here we actually assume no re-education experience for all individuals. Namely, no individual receives any further education once they start working. We believe it is an acceptable scenario for older people (e.g., aged 30 and above). Younger people (e.g., aged between 15 and 16), however, are far more likely to get re-enrolled some years after dropout or pursue higher levels of education. That is, the average years of schooling of individuals aged 18 when surveyed in 2005 may be longer than that of individuals aged 15 in 2002 (though the former is the best representative of the latter).Nevertheless, we still make such an assumption due to the following three reasons. First, the 15–64 age groups are classified as working-age population by the United Nations and the commonly used dependency ratios are subsequently defined. This implicitly assumes that individuals over 15 do not re-enter the education system, otherwise this group will be excluded from the labor force (not willing to work). Second, the idea that individuals entering the work force at the age of 15 is roughly consistent with Chinese's education pattern. Most Chinese start primary school at the age of 6, move on to secondary school at the age 12, and then attain secondary education (compulsory) at the age of 15. Third, if we know the average age when people in each province start working (e.g., the age of 18), we can easily apply the aforementioned analysis to a different definition of working-age population (e.g., aged 18–64). In other words, we make such simplified assumptions owning to data limitations, but it can be readily modified when more data is available.

13 See Bai *et al.* (2006, 2007) for more details. We update Bai's and his colleagues' estimates with the latest data from the NBS website and most recently published yearbooks. Note that instead of summing the capital stock of construction and

installation and that of equipment as done by Bai *et al.* (2006, 2007), we can alternatively estimate the physical capital stock directly with annual aggregate investment data. We prove that these two approaches are theoretically equivalent if the deflator used for aggregate investment is the weighted harmonic mean of the deflators of construction and installation investment and equipment investment. They, however, may be empirically different since the price index of aggregate investment includes investment that cannot be grouped into construction and installation investment and that of equipment.

14 We compare our estimates of these two series with those obtained by other scholars such as Perkins and Rawski (2008) and find them to be very similar despite the differences in data, estimating methods, and indicators. Only some minor differences exist in terms of years of beginning (possibly due to different assumptions of initial physical capital stock) and ending (possibly due to data later modified by the NBS).

15 Significant productivity differences among these sectors are well documented in the literature.

16 Provincial GRP and national GDP of the United States are both valued in 2005 prices in US dollars. We first get the annual USD/CNY bid and ask rates based on data of China's GDP respectively valued in RMB and USD (both are in 2005 prices) from the UN data website. The data of provincial GRP per capita valued in RMB are then accordingly converted into those in USD. The annual GDP per capita data in 2005 prices for the United States are calculated with data of GDP (from the UN data website) divided by data of aggregate population (from the OECD website). This means we always assume the United States as the productivity frontier. Some may prefer to consider another CUI, the productivity level for each province relative to the United States. We here for simplicity follow Lucas (2009) to consider the CUI of relative income levels. The results, which are not presented here but are available upon request, with the alternative CUI of relative productivities are similar.

17 The NBS website publishes two data series of exports and imports since 1993; one is recorded according to the jurisdictions where the domestic firms are registered and the other is classified by the commodity's region of origin and destination. We carefully compare these two series with data from *The Compendium of Statistical Data and Materials on 50 Years of New China* and find that the former is more comparable with the compendium data and therefore choose it for combining the final series between 1978 and 2014.

18 It is worth mentioning that the way of obtaining annual USD/CNY bid and ask rates for converting imports and exports vary slightly from the way of those for converting provincial GRP. This is because we think the former is mainly related to tradable goods, whereas the latter is used for all goods (including tradable and non-tradable ones).

19 Measuring government size could be a daunting task. Some recommend the use of the ratio of local government expenditure to provincial GRP as a proxy. This method is not considered here for two reasons. First, these two measures are very similar since local government income approximately equals local government expenditure for all provinces in all years. The second is that part of the central government spending, such as funding for certain agricultural irrigation projects, targets only one or several provinces. It should be included in the local government expenditure of the benefiting provinces, though they are currently

not. Such detailed data are not publicly available and exploration in this area, though meaningful, is beyond the scope of this study. Therefore we choose to ignore the nuances for simplicity.

20 Measuring the impact of non-budgetary expenditures (which also play a significant role in boosting local economic growth) on TFP, though important, is well beyond the scope of this study, owing to the lack of comparable datasets.

21 An alternative is to define the economic weight of SOEs as the proportion of industrial output by SOEs out of total industrial output. Both indicators only partly represent the relative size of SOEs in the Chinese economy (measuring only the size of investment, in the former case, and the industrial output, in the latter, by firms large enough to be surveyed).

22 Note that both indicators contain inter- and intra-provincial migration. A much more reasonable way is to establish three indicators to distinguish between intra-provincial migration rate, immigration rate, and emigration rate. Unfortunately, we do not have access to the relevant data.

23 Commonly used LLC (Levin *et al.*, 2002), IPS (Im *et al.*, 2003), and Hadri (Hadri, 2000) tests can all be applied to unit root tests on panel data. The null hypothesis is the some panels contain unit roots for LLC test, all panels contain unit roots for IPS test, and all panels are stationary for Hadri test, respectively. However, the LLC and Hadri tests require a strictly balanced panel, which is unsatisfied here since observations for certain indicators are missing in some provinces in some years.

24 This implies lower productivity growth rates for the primary and tertiary industries. The former is naturally expected and the latter may be partly due to its inclusion of some sectors with lower productivity such as public administration and social service institutions.

25 That is, the natural logarithm of relative lagged real GDP per capita of China to lagged real GDP per capita of the United States. For estimation methods and data source, see the previous discussion.

26 We choose the 2001 to 2014 time horizon because it can be conveniently divided into two intervals of the same length: 2001 to 2007 (before 2008) and 2008 to 2014 (after 2008). The four indicators are chosen because their estimated coefficients are statistically significant. For estimation methods and data source, see the previous discussion.

27 For example, a change in investment rate in 2008 would cause a change in TFP in 2008; therefore the GDP in 2008 would change. The new GDP would further predict a new TFP in 2009 since TFP growth rate in 2009 is related to GDP in 2008, as implied by convergence theory, and then the GDP in 2009 would also change.

28 We cannot get corresponding estimators for time dummies at the national level, but the cyclical pattern of which can be approximated by estimated time dummies from the provincial panel (though most of them are statistically insignificant in all columns of Table 2.2). It is worth noting that the means of the indicators in Table 2.2 for the national time series and the provincial panel are not exactly the same; therefore we show the actual observations on the left axis and the "with" and "without time trend" curves on the right vertical axis in Figure 2.2. This is to better show the trend of these curves without affecting the final conclusion.

29 The GDP value obtained here could affect capital output ratio and, in turn, its growth rate. For this reason, instead of using the growth accounting equation, we adopt the goal-seeking method to find a GDP to solve the equation for each year.

30 Recall that GDP as measured by the expenditure approach equals C (consumption) plus I (investment, or capital formation) plus G (government spending) plus NX (net exports). These two assumptions are consistent with the CFA on investment rate, where the government size and trade dependency ratio both take their actual values for all the years from 2008 to 2014.

3   Policy implications

Findings in the first part of this study show that, on one hand, as the gap in economic development level between China and the United States narrows, the potential growth rate of labor productivity has been showing a continuously downward trend over the projection period; on the other hand, due to the decline in employment participation rates as a result of aging population, there will be a decrease in labor force growth rate, or even negative growth, in future years. On average, as the potential growth rate of labor productivity and labor force decreases, China's potential growth rate will experience a continuous decline: 6.29% over the period of 2016 to 2020, 5.54% over 2021 to 2025, 4.84% over 2026 to 2030, 3.96% over 2031 to 2035, 3.31% over 2036 to 2040, 3.33% over 2041 to 2045, and 2.90% over 2046 to 2050.

Results of the analysis on factors determining productivity changes in China in the second part of this study suggest that, first, from the technical efficiency point of view, the level of openness to the outside world has a significant and positive impact on productivity, whereas relative income level has a significant and negative impact. Second, from the factor utilization efficiency point of view, non-productive investment accumulation and employment participation rate affect the efficient use of factors and generate negative and positive impact on productivity, respectively. Third, from the factor allocation efficiency point of view, both government intervention and investment rate have a significantly negative impact on productivity. In sum, China's recent productivity decline is largely due to the weakening of "latecomer advantages" and a rising investment rate.

In addition, China's superior growth performance between 2009 and 2011 over other economies benefited, to a certain extent, from the aggressive stimulus package China adopted in response to the financial crisis. The stimulus package helped to mitigate the shocks of the financial crisis and the European sovereign-debt crisis in the short run; yet it could not reverse the long-term trend of declining economic growth. As a result of large-scale government investment, the tax burden on capital fell, while the tax burden on labor rose after the financial crisis. "Equipment investment," which is more conducive to economy growth, dropped sharply, whereas less-efficient state sectors received more investment. These have had adverse impacts on the overall productivity and restricted the growth of residents' consumption expenditures. When the stimulus package expired, its "growth stabilizing" effect faded quickly, but its negative impact on productivity lingered on.

The above-mentioned findings show that China's economic slowdown is a long-term trend. It is a structural change caused by a decrease in potential growth after China entered into the economic new normal, rather than cyclical fluctuations of real growth rates caused by short-term external shocks. Based on the current trends of labor force and labor productivity growth, it appears to be quite difficult for China's GDP to double in size from the 2010 level by the end of the 13th Five-Year Plan. Recommendations include speeding up supply-side structural reform, implementing macroeconomic policy frameworks to effectively address the issue of decline in both labor and labor productivity growth. Detailed policy suggestions are outlined below.

Adapt to a lower growth potential

It is an inevitable long-term trend that China's economy shifts gear from high growth to a medium-to-high growth, which is essentially a process of restructuring the economy and finding new drivers of growth. China should act proactively to adapt to the new normal and make sure its economy runs within a reasonable range, gradually reduce demand-side management and emergency stabilization measures, focus more on achieving structural balance through supply-side reforms, stress the role of innovation as a key growth driver, and give prominence to the quality and efficiency of economic growth.

Our previous analysis has shown that China's economic growth rate exceeded its potential growth rate during 2009 to 2011, mainly because of the rapid increase in investment. During this period, however, the efficiency of economic growth was relatively low. We found that the average growth rate of total factor productivity (TFP) was less than half of the rate before 2008, and return on investment decreased continuously as well. Our research further revealed that a major cause for the slowdown in TFP growth rate was the excessive investment driven by fiscal stimulus. Such investment was resource intensive and less efficient. It raised the capital and labor cost for production activities with relatively higher efficiency, inhibiting these activities and further reducing the overall efficiency in the economy. Rapid growth driven by accelerated investment is unsustainable.

Sustainable economic growth can only be achieved through continuous improvement in efficiency. Excessive investment led to low ROI and high investment cost. Needless to say, China's fiscal capacity simply cannot afford to support such high levels of investment going forward. The resultant rapid upsurge in government debt would increase hidden risks in the economy.

Shift the focus of existing fiscal policy

Fiscal policy should continue to be proactive. However, it should switch focus from increasing spending to cutting taxes. When stimulus-oriented investments are used to create demand in industries with excessive capacity, more resources will be consumed, resulting in a rise in resource prices as well as labor and capital costs for more efficient sectors. Thus, to solve issues associated with structural adjustments, the government should pay attention to preventing the crowding-out effect, steadily cut stimulus-oriented investments, and reduce factor cost. We also suggest that local debt should be better controlled. At present, there is a prevailing belief among investors that the central government will come to the rescue of local government facing debt crisis. Such expectation would no doubt cloud their financial judgments. How to break such expectation and control local debt growth is a major issue. Although China's budget law prohibits local government from providing guarantees for financing platforms, in practice, financial institutions still think this is the case. The government should strictly enforce the budget law to change this situation.

In terms of cost reduction, priority should be given to the reduction of social security payment rates. We recommend the government deal with the leftover issues of China's basic pension insurance scheme and the setting of the pension insurance payment rate separately. The former can be solved by allocating states assets and the dividends from the state-owned enterprises to fill the deficits. Once those historical leftovers are resolved, the government could strictly follow the actuarial balance principle in setting the payment rate so as to keep the discounted value of lifetime payment the same with that of the lifetime benefits enjoyed by the new generation of insurance participants; such payment rate is significantly lower than the current one. China's current basic pension insurance payment rate is very high, which can be attributed largely to the historical burdens. The high payment rate and the setting of such high payment rate to raise funds for the purpose of solving the historical issues have created a lot of problems. First, it seriously affects firms' competitiveness. A main contributor to the high cost facing Chinese firms is the exorbitant pension insurance rate. Second, it reduces employees' disposable income, which in turn hinders their consumption.

As many studies have shown, high social security payment rate is one of the primary factors that drive down disposable income, whereas the slow growth in disposable income is the main cause that drives down consumption. Third, it intensifies payment evasion. Studies have shown that higher payment rates correspond with more severe payment evasion. Forth, it is unfair. Pension insurance payment is regressive. Because there are both floor and ceiling to the social insurance payment base, employees with salary below the floor actually pay at an above-average rate, whereas those with salary above the ceiling pay at a below-average rate. It is extremely unfair to raise funds using the regressive contribution method in order to make up the shortfall left over from the basic insurance program.

Given that the historical leftovers stem mostly from ensuring the pension payments to SOE retirees who contributed to the accumulation of state-owned capital, it is only fair and reasonable to allocate state-owned capital and dividends to solve the issues. The government should use state-owned capital or the return for the retirement benefits. Allocating part of the state-owned capital to the social security fund will not affect SOEs' public ownership. It can even improve corporate governance and help strengthen China's basic economic system.

To solve the historical issues for good, there should be a systematic estimation of future payments to the retired, as well as the share of payments made to the retired that are contributed by those yet to retire. These are the two major components of the historical leftovers. Considerations should be given to the accrued return on pension contributions made by workers yet to retire.

Once the leftover issues are solved, the contribution rate for basic pension insurance will drop significantly. Reducing the contribution rate helps to raise the collection rate. As a result, the decrease in the actual contribution would be smaller than the decrease in contribution rate. Moreover, reducing the contribution rate could help the government win more social support for postponing the retirement age. The reduction of the contribution rate for basic pension insurance will make room for the second and the third pillars of pension insurance. The three pillars will be able to safeguard a reasonable pension replacement rate. At the same time, the government would be able to provide better benefits without raising the payment rate by improving investment management for social security funds and raising the return on investment. It is entirely feasible to cut the payment rate to 20% and firms' cost burden would be greatly reduced. As long as the leftover issues are solved in the transition period and the reduced payment rate satisfies actuarial equivalent requirement, cutting the rate will not generate adverse impacts on the long-term fiscal sustainability of China's social security funds. Turnover tax rates in China such as the corporate income tax rate and the value added tax rate, on the other hand, are quite reasonable; cutting these tax rates may affect the government's long-term fiscal sustainability. Thus, lowering the social security payment rate is more practical and reasonable than lowering various tax rates levied on firms.

Further streamlining administration, delegating authority to appropriate levels, and reducing or eliminating various administrative fees is another important step towards minimizing firms' burdens. It would boost business vitality and thereby promote economic growth. Charges for services firms do not need or for repetitive services provided by different departments present a huge waste. The government should straighten out these administrative items and cut down or even abolish unreasonable charges. This requires concerted efforts at both central and local levels, since local governments cannot manage this task alone as some of the charges are made by the central government or its directly subordinate units.

In addition, with accelerated population aging, decrease in labor force will be one of the key factors pushing down China's future economic growth. Putting more effort into investing in people to raise labor productivity can be an effective long-term mechanism for achieving sustainable economic growth. Following the requirements of "broad coverage, basic needs, good quality," the government should commit more fiscal resources to pre-school and compulsory education, giving priority to the remote, rural, poor, and minority areas and ensuring reasonably affordable access for orphans, children from poor families, and children with disabilities. Furthermore, efforts should be made to reduce the number of students in a class, distribute teacher resources reasonably, promote the sharing of high-quality resources, and further advance the balanced development of basic education.

Resolve the issue of excess industrial capacity

Efforts to reduce excess capacity should follow the principle of "market-driven, firms-led, organized locally, supported at the central level with a comprehensive set of policy instruments" and focus on addressing the root causes. One such root cause is the continued lending by the financial sector to zombie firms, which is believed to be responsible for the economic woes that have befallen Japan since the 1990s. We recommend that, first and foremost, the social role of financial institutions and financial markets should be restricted mainly to improving the efficiency of resource allocation and controlling financial risks, and fiscal and monetary policies should be relied on more to provide other social responsibilities. This way, the costs are more transparent and there is less risk. A moderate fiscal policy stance should be adopted so as to avoid crowding out market activities and at the same time raise the cost of zombie lending. Second, financial institutions should be given stronger incentives to improve their capital allocation. They should be encouraged to expand capital reserves so that the exposure to non-performing loans will not affect their capability to meet regulatory requirements on capital adequacy. Moreover, unreasonable current-term profit targets should not be set for financial institutions; otherwise they would be prompted to conceal the true size of their non-performing loans. By helping financial institutions about to violate regulatory requirements to detect and write off non-performing loans and supplement capital resources, they would be more willing to expose and deal with bad debts. At the same time, the government should reinforce the implementation of lending practices based on risk-based loan classifications. Third, local government interventions in the decision-making of financial institutions should be reduced and, in particular, they should be allowed more autonomy in dealing with non-performing loans. Cutting zombie lending is key to achieving sustainable growth. The independence of financial institutions should be improved to ensure they make sound investment choices based on market conditions and their own situations. This is the key prerequisite for solving China's investment structure problem. The continued presence of zombie firms not only impairs efficiency directly, but also reduces growth space for other firms and the willingness of financial institutions to provide loans for them which results in less-efficient investment. Fourth, strong support should be given to improve financial institutions' access to information. Regulatory authority should enforce stricter information disclosure requirements for firms seeking financing so as to facilitate sound lending decision-making. Fifth, local debts need to be put under better control. Currently, there is a prevailing belief among investors that the central government will come to the rescue of local governments facing debt crisis, which obviously clouds their financial judgments. How to effectively break such expectations and control local debt growth remain key issues.

The government should reduce overcapacity through market competition, give financial support to highly competitive firms with good returns, and effectively cut off channels for zombie firms in industries with severe overcapacity to access funds through loans, debt issuance, and listing. Loans should be made available to firms engaged in industrial consolidation. Furthermore, the financial market should play a more active role in facilitating firms' mergers and acquisitions (M&A) aimed at reducing overcapacity, as well as offer innovative financial products and services to support firms' post M&A product upgrading and technological innovation. The formation of industrial leaders and market-oriented resources allocation should be facilitated and favorable institutional conditions for market-oriented bankruptcy should be created. Orderly exits should be facilitated by speeding up bankruptcy and liquidation trials and allowing legal proceedings to fully perform the functions of phasing out obsolete firms and capacity. Additionally, firms should be guided and encouraged to absorb more laid-off and unemployed workers through fiscal instruments such as tax incentives and reducing the social impact of structural adjustments.

Large-scale firm exits in industries with excess capacity may cause a series of social problems. Therefore, the compensation mechanism should be improved. We recommend that the government set up special compensation funds and firm exit aid funds, build a robust social security system, make proper arrangements for the laid-off workers, ensure the most basic obligation towards those effected are fulfilled, and protect the legal rights of workers from the exit firms.

Market system reform

The core and direction of supply-side reform is the supply of a market-oriented system. China needs to break away from the government-led allocation model in which the government plays a predominate role in the distribution of key resource factors such as land and capital. The importance of market self-adjustment should be stressed and institutional innovations in factor markets should be facilitated. The optimal allocation of capital and labor across departments should be guided by product and factor price reforms.

In terms of SOE reform, the role of government should be gradually transformed from managing SOEs to managing state-owned capital. In particular, focus should be placed on strengthening the supervision of state-owned assets, improving capital allocation and operational efficiency, and pushing forward with the strategic adjustment of the state-owned sector. Traditional SOEs with severe overcapacity and limited growth potential should be bankrupted in accordance with relevant laws so as to optimize the supply side of the economy. In addition, we suggest the government institutionalize the protection against state asset loss at the top political and legal level to reduce the gaming of the system. Laws and regulations protecting state-owned assets should be refined and the procedural rules governing the transfer of state property should be improved. Furthermore, the fairness and soundness of related transactions should be emphasized. Anti-corruption efforts should be intensified and the free flow of upward communication through external supervision channels should be ensured.

To achieve structural transformation, the government should guide the flow of factors from low efficiency sectors to high efficiency sectors. In addition, existing assets should be revitalized. As a lot of assets are severely under-utilized at present, improving their utilization rate could free up resources for the formation of new supplies. In the process of realizing the optimal allocation of factors, attention should be paid to the policy risks for the M&A between firms of mixed ownership and firms of different ownerships. The key mechanism is to guarantee the rights and interests of private enterprises at the institutional level; remove institutional and policy obstacles and entry barriers; and build an open, transparent, and standardized market entrance. Existing restrictive or even discriminatory policies toward private players should be reformed and unfair competition should be reduced by eliminating institutional factors that result in different factor costs for firms of different ownerships. Meanwhile, the government should reduce differences in entry barriers for firms of different ownerships: industrial sectors and business domains where investments are not explicitly prohibited by laws or regulations should be open to firms of different ownerships.

Deepening the streamlining of administration and decentralization; promoting transparency and openness in government, judiciary, and law enforcement; fully implementing the government power list, regulation list, and negative list system; shifting from quantitative decentralization to open market; and reducing transaction costs arising from institutional factors continuously should all be pursued.

In terms of opening up, only a handful of service areas (e.g., health care and aged care) are currently accessible to foreign investment. In this respect, China is lagging behind the international standard. The government should provide better conditions regarding market access in order to attract foreign investment in these areas and enable domestic institutions to gain managerial experience and talent from foreign firms.

Reduce housing inventory through new types of urbanization and labor efficiency improvements

Our research has shown that urbanization is a key determinant of efficient factor use; meanwhile, high-quality urbanization is an effective means of increasing overall demand. To date, *hukou* and land issues remain the main obstacle to Chin's urbanization. As such, abolishing the household registration system, allowing rural migrants to move freely to cities, and solving the education problem for their children should be placed high on China's reform agenda. Meanwhile, addressing land issues as a result of massive migration to urban areas should also be prioritized. Urbanization can only be further advanced when land, *hukou*, and welfare issues are solved.

Apart from providing rural migrants with equal access to public service and welfare, more measures are needed to help their integration into the urban communities. If rural migrants have more disposable income and property, they will be more likely to afford housing purchases in the cities. This in turn helps to expand effective demand, connect demand and supply, reduce housing overstock, stabilize the real estate market, and create more demand for the home renovation market. Meanwhile, more disposable properties would allow rural migrants to, for example, gain access to better social security and spend more on pension, medical and unemployment insurance.

Peasants' rural properties typically consist of homestead and land contract rights. Chongqing's land ticket scheme and other similar programs are effective measures that help peasants mobilize and liquidize their homestead rights. If the government allows peasants to sell their homestead lands or to transfer their land contract rights to a larger population, the value of these assets could be further increased. Nevertheless, caution should be exerted in the above-mentioned process with regard to the pace and intensity of reforms. The government should also put in place a complementary set of institutions and regulate intermediaries and legal services so as to prevent a rush to sell and the resultant drop in the market value of the limited assets peasants own.

The government should incorporate the above-mentioned two considerations when pushing forward the urbanization of household registration and welfare provision. Furthermore, the government should set a clear direction for further housing reforms. Likewise, it should expand the coverage of the public rental housing scheme to people without urban *hukou*, encourage real estate developers to cut prices, and abolish outdated restrictive measures with the goals of meeting the housing demand of new citizens and setting up a housing system suitable for both purchasing and renting needs. The development of rental housing companies and the use of houses that are already built or to be built for rental purposes, supporting homeowners to rent out private properties, and permitting the conversion of commercial building into rental houses should all be encouraged. In addition, the government should monetize public rental housing and provide subsidies to those who are eligible to rent in the market. Promoting the development of the rental housing market can lower market entrance costs and alleviate the pressure of house purchasing by breaking long-term repayments into short-term rental payments, which can further unleash demands. Moreover, land policies should be tailored to the specific situations of different cities. For small- and medium-sized cities with ballooning inventories, the main direction should be reducing real estate stock. The government could encourage firms to relocate to areas with extensive stock in order to create jobs and facilitate real estate de-stocking while achieving balanced economic development through industry development and city-industry integration.

In the process of urbanization, to improve efficiency through agglomeration, the government should encourage population migration to medium-sized cities other than mega-cities. Many studies have shown that agglomeration effects can bring about a significant improvement in efficiency. Research has also found that apart from mega-cities, cities in China have yet to reach a scale at which they can fully benefit from agglomeration effects. Japan experienced very rapid economic growth during 1950 to 1973, a period in which there were mass population movements into big cities. In the early 1970s, Japan started to implement the "Policy for Balanced Growth of State-owned Land" and provided all sorts of subsidies to rural areas, which slowed the concentration of population to big cities. The rate of economic growth in Japan declined subsequently.

China's subsidies for agriculture, rural areas, and peasants have contributed greatly to their development. However, China's agriculture has entered a stage of high costs, high risks, and tightening resources and environment constraints. With the continued growth of China's fiscal capacity, the type of agricultural subsidy and its share in fiscal allocation could also be increased accordingly. The government should fully exert its macro-control and public service functions in adjusting and optimizing agricultural subsidy policies with the basic objectives of ensuring food security and efficient supply of major agricultural products, fostering a new agricultural management system and management body, facilitating the change in production methods, and raising rural incomes. By improving the direction and focus of the subsidies programs, as well as the dual roles of subsidies in stimulating production and increasing income, the government can push forward agricultural modernization.

The government should also encourage the relocation of traditional industries and the flow of production and market factors to Midwestern regions, as well as guide rural migrant workers from these areas to seek employment in local counties through a series of fiscal, tax, and credit incentives. Once these migrant workers have regular income and social security, the government can reclaim their land and rural houses and pay a certain amount of compensation for them to buy houses in towns and cities. Meanwhile, the government could rent the reclaimed land to large farm operators so as to realize intensive management of agriculture, cost reductions, and increases in farmers' income.

Financial reform

Another important phenomenon as China enters the period of medium and low growth is the gradual exposure of financial risks in the Chinese economy. During the previous investment-driven stage of development, the government has set too many targets for financial institutions and financial markets. We suggest that there should be a return to the most fundamental function of finance – the primary responsibility of financial institutions and financial markets are to effectively allocate resources and control financial risks. Optimizing factor and rescue allocation and controlling financial risks are the best support the financial sector can provide to promote long-term economic growth. Financial institutions could play a role in stabilizing short-term growth under the guidance of fiscal and monetary policies, rather than acting in the latter's place. Greater independence should be given to financial institutions and financial markets if they are to do their work. Moreover, the government should strengthen financial regulation and supervision at all levels.

Credit default should be dealt with in accordance with laws and regulations, all kinds of financing activities should be regulated, targeted financial risk mitigation programs should be carried out, and the monitoring and early warning of financial risks should be strengthened. We recommend that the government continues to deepen financial reforms, accelerate the reform of China's investment and financing system, eliminate the institutional basis for the generation and amplification of financial risks, and further promote economic deleveraging. At the same time, the government should strengthen the implementation of deposit insurance system, facilitate asset securitization, increase banks' asset turnover ratio, and liquidize their capital reserves so as to accelerate the dilution of financial risks. Moreover, as the "impossible trinity" theory dictates, independence of monetary policy, free flow of capital, and stable exchange rates cannot be realized at the same time. While maintaining the independence of monetary policy and overall quantity control, we recommend that the government pay close attention to the adverse impacts of exchange rate fluctuations on real economy and asset price stability during the regime reform and steadily promote RMB internationalization.

References

Abramovitz, M. Resource and Output Trends in the United States Since 1870. *American Economic Review Papers and Proceedings*, 1956, 46: 1–23.

Aigner, D., Lovell, C. A., and Schmidt, P. Formulation and Estimation of Stochastic Frontier Production Function Models. *Journal of Econometrics*, 1977, 6(1): 21–37.

Aizenman, J., and Spiegel, M. M. Takeoffs. *Review of Development Economics*, 2010, 14(2): 177–196.

Arrow, K. J. The Economic Implications of Learning by Doing. *The Review of Economic Studies*, 1962, 29(3): 155–173.

Bai, C. E., Hsieh, C. T., and Qian, Y. Y. The Return to Capital in China. *Brookings Papers on Economic Activity*, 2006, 2: 61–88.

Bai, C. E., Hsieh, C. T., and Qian, Y. Y. The Return to Capital in China. *Comparative Studies* (in Chinese), 2007, 28: 1–22.

Bai, C. E., Li, D., Tao, Z. G., and Wang, Y. J. A Multi-Task Theory of the State Enterprise Reform. *Journal of Comparative Economics*, 2000, 28(4): 716–738.

Bai, C. E., and Zhang, Q. Revealing the Unknown With the Known: Implications for Total Factor Productivity Researches in China. *China Finance Review* (in Chinese), 2014, 1: 135–151.

Banerjee, A. V., and Duflo, E. Growth Theory Through the Lens of Development Economics. *Handbook of Economic Growth*, 2005, 1: 473–552.

Barro, R. J. Notes on Growth Accounting. *Journal of Economic Growth*, 1999, 4(2): 119–137.

Barro, R. J., and Sala-i-Martin, X. *Economic Growth* (2nd Edition). Cambridge, MA, MIT Press, 1995.

Benhabib, J., and Spiegel, M. M. The Role of Human Capital in Economic Development Evidence From Aggregate Cross-Country Data. *Journal of Monetary Economics*, 1994, 34(2): 143–173.

Brandt, L., Ma, D. B., and Rawski, T. G. From Divergence to Convergence: Re-Evaluating the History Behind China's Economic Boom [R]. Working Paper No.117. Coventry, UK: Department of Economics, University of Warwick, 2013. (CAGE Online Working Paper Series). Available at http://wrap.warwick.ac.uk/57944.

Brandt, L., Van Biesebroeck, J., and Zhang, Y. Creative Accounting or Creative Destruction? Firm-level Productivity Growth in Chinese Manufacturing. *Journal of Development Economics*, 2012, 97(2): 339–351.

Cai, F. How Can Chinese Economy Achieve the Transition Toward Total Factor Productivity Growth? *Social Science in China* (in Chinese), 2013, 1: 56–71.

Cai, F. A Supply-side Prospect to Understand China's Economic Slowdown. *Economic Perspectives* (in Chinese), 2016, 4: 14–22.

Cai, F., and Lu, Y. Population Change and Resulting Slowdown in Potential GDP Growth in China. *China & World Economy*, 2013a, 21(2): 1–14.

Cai, F., and Lu, Y. What Potential Growth Rate Can China Accomplish in the Future Ten Years? *Globalization* (in Chinese), 2013b, 1: 27–37.

Caves, D. W., Christensen, L. R., and Diewert, W. E. The Economic Theory of Index Numbers and the Measurement of Input, Output, and Productivity. *Econometrica*, 1982, 50(6): 1393–1414.

Charnes, A., Cooper, W. W., and Rhodes, E. Measuring the Efficiency of Decision Making Units. *European Journal of Operational Research*, 1978, 2(6): 429–444.

Chen, K., Wang, H., Zheng, Y., Jefferson, G. H., and Rawski, T. G. Productivity Change in Chinese Industry: 1953–1985. *Journal of Comparative Economics*, 1988, 12(4): 570–591.

Chen, Z., Lu, M., and Jin, Y. Regional Differences of Human Capital and Education Development in China: An Estimation of the Panel Data. *The Journal of World Economy* (in Chinese), 2004, 12: 25–31.

Chow, G. C. Capital Formation and Economic Growth in China. *The Quarterly Journal of Economics*, 1993, 108(3): 809–842.

Chow, G. C., and Li, K. W. China's Economic Growth: 1952–2010. *Economic Development and Cultural Change*, 2002, 51(1): 247–256.

Christensen, L. R., and Jorgenson, D. W. The Measurement of US Real Capital Input, 1929–1967. *Review of Income and Wealth*, 1969, 15(4): 293–320.

Christensen, L. R., and Jorgenson, D. W. US Real Product and Real Factor Input, 1929–1967. *Review of Income and Wealth*, 1970, 16(1): 19–50.

Denison, E. F. *Why Growth Rates Differ: Postwar Experience in Nine Western Countries*. Washington, DC, Washington Brookings Institution, 1967.

Denison, E. F. Classification of Sources of Growth. *Review of Income and Wealth*, 1972, 18(1): 1–25.

Eichengreen, B., Park, D., and Shin, K. When Fast Growing Economies Slow Down: International Evidence and Implications for China [R]. National Bureau of Economic Research Working Paper No.w16919, 2011.

Eichengreen, B., Park, D., and Shin, K. When Fast-Growing Economies Slow Down: International Evidence and Implications for China. *Asian Economic Papers*, 2012, 11(1): 42–87.

Eichengreen, B., Park, D., and Shin, K. Growth Slowdowns Redux: New Evidence on the Middle-income Trap. National Bureau of Economic Research Working Paper w18673, 2013.

Farrell, M. J. The Measurement of Productive Efficiency. *Journal of the Royal Statistical Society. Series A (General)*, 1957, 120(3): 253–290.

The Forecast and Analysis of Economic Situation Research Team at the Chinese Academy of Social Sciences. *Economic Blue Books: Economy of China Analysis and Forecast (2013)*. Beijing: Social Sciences Academic Press, 2012.

The Forecast and Analysis of Economic Situation Research Team at the Chinese Academy of Social Sciences. *Economic Blue Books: Economy of China Analysis and Forecast (2014)*. Beijing: Social Sciences Academic Press, 2013.

The Forecast and Analysis of Economic Situation Research Team at the Chinese Academy of Social Sciences. *Economic Blue Books: Economy of China Analysis and Forecast (2015)*. Beijing: Social Sciences Academic Press, 2014.

The Forecast and Analysis of Economic Situation Research Team at the Chinese Academy of Social Sciences. *Economic Blue Books: Economy of China Analysis and Forecast (2016)*. Beijing: Social Sciences Academic Press, 2015.

Frankel, J. Globalization and Chinese Growth: Ends of Trends? HKS Working Paper No. 16–029, 2016. Available at https://papers.ssrn.com/sol3/papers.cfm?abstract_id=2820766.

Goldsmith, R. W. A Perpetual Inventory of National Wealth. *Studies in Income and Wealth*, NBER, 1951, 14: 5–74.

Grossman, G. M., and Helpman, E. Trade, Knowledge Spillovers, and Growth. *European Economic Review*, 1991, 35(2): 517–526.

Hadri, K. Testing for Stationarity in Heterogeneous Panel Data. *Econometrics Journal*, 2000, 3: 148–161.

He, Y. Q. Openness and TFP Growth: An Empirical Study Based on the Inter-Provincial Panel Data in China. *China Economic Quarterly* (in Chinese), 2007, 6(4): 1127–1142.

Holz, C. China's Economic Growth 1978–2025: What We Know Today About China's Economic Growth Tomorrow. *World Development*, 2008, 36(10): 1665–1691.

Hsieh, C. T., and Klenow, P. J. Misallocation and Manufacturing TFP in China and India. *The Quarterly Journal of Economics*, 2009, 124(4): 1403–1448.

Huang, Y., Fang, C., Peng, X., and Gou, Q. The New Normal of Chinese Development. In *China: A New Model for Growth and Development* (edited by Ross Garnaut, Fang Cai, and Ligang Song). Canberra, The Australian National University E Press, 2013: 35–54.

Im, K. S., Pesaran, M. H., and Shin, Y. Testing for Unit Roots in Heterogeneous Panels. *Journal of Econometrics*, 2003, 115(1): 53–74.

Johansson, Å., Guillemette, Y., Murtin, F., Turner, D., Nicoletti, G., de la Maisonneuve, C., Bousquet, G., and Spinelli, F. Looking to 2060: Long-Term Global Growth Prospects. OECD Economic Policy Papers No.03, 2012.

Jones, C. I. Misallocation, Economic Growth, and Input-Output Economics. National Bureau of Economic Research Working Paper w16742, 2011.

Jorgenson, D. W., and Griliches, Z. The Explanation of Productivity Change. *The Review of Economic Studies*, 1967, 34(3): 249–283.

Leibenstein, H. Allocative Efficiency vs. "X-efficiency". *The American Economic Review*, 1966, 56(3): 392–415.

Levin, A., Lin, C. F., and Chu, C. S. Unit Root Tests in Panel Data: Asymptotic and Finite-Sample Properties. *Journal of Econometrics*, 2002, 108(1): 1–24.

Liu, S. J. *China's Economic Outlook in Ten Years (2013–2022): Looking for the New Driving Force and the Balance*. Beijing, China Citic Press, 2013.

74   *References*

Liu, S. J. *China's Economic Outlook in Ten Years (2014–2023): New Normal of Growth in Reform*. Beijing, China Citic Press, 2014.

Liu, S. J. *China's Economic Outlook in Ten Years (2015–2024): Scale the Highland of Efficiency*. Beijing, China Citic Press, 2015.

Lu, Y., and Cai, F. Effects of Adjusting Population Policy on China's Long-run Potential Economic Growth Rate. *Studies in Labor Economics* (in Chinese), 2013, 1: 35–50.

Lu, Y., and Cai, F. Effects of Demographic Transition on Potential Economic Growth Rate: Comparing China to Japan. *The Journal of World Economy* (in Chinese), 2014, 1: 3–29.

Lu, Y., and Cai, F. From Demographic Dividend to Reform Dividend: A Simulation Based on China's Potential Economic Growth Rate. *The Journal of World Economy* (in Chinese), 2016, 1: 3–23.

Lucas, R. E. Why Doesn't Capital Flow from Rich to Poor Countries? *The American Economic Review*, 1990, 80(2): 92–96.

Lucas, R. E. Trade and the Diffusion of the Industrial Revolution. *American Economic Journal: Macroeconomics*, 2009, 1(1):1–25.

Luo, D. M., Li, Y., and Shi, J. C. Factor Distortion, Misallocation and Productivity. *Economic Research Journal* (in Chinese), 2012, 3: 4–14.

MacDougall, G. D. A. The Benefits and Costs of Private Investment from Abroad: A Theoretical Approach. *Bulletin of the Oxford University Institute of Economics & Statistics*, 1960, 22(3): 189–211.

Maddison, A. Statistics on World Population, GDP and Per Capita GDP, 1–2008 AD. Historical Statistics, 2010: 1–36.

Mankiw, N. G., Romer, D., and Weil, D. N. A Contribution to the Empirics of Economic Growth. *The Quarterly Journal of Economics*, 1992, 107(2): 407–437.

Nelson, R. R., and Phelps, E. S. Investment in Humans, Technological Diffusion, and Economic Growth. *The American Economic Review*, 1966, 56(1/2): 69–75.

Perkins, D. H., and Rawski, T. G. Forecasting China's Economic Growth to 2025. In *China's Great Economic Transformation* (edited by Loren Brandt and Thomas G. Rawski). Cambridge, Cambridge University Press, 2008: 829–886.

Prasad, E. S. Is the Chinese Growth Miracle Built to Last? *China Economic Review*, 2009, 20(1): 103–123.

Pritchett, L., and Summers, L. H. Asiaphoria Meets Regression to the Mean. National Bureau of Economic Research Working Paper No. 20573, 2014.

Qu, H. B. How is China's Potential Economic Growth Rate? *China Reform* (in Chinese), 2015, 1–2: 19–26.

Quesnay, F. *The Economic Table – Tableau Economique*. New York, Gordon Press, 1766/1973.

Ren, R. E., and Liu, X. S. Some Problems With Estimating Capital Stock in China. *The Journal of Quantitative & Technical Economics* (in Chinese), 1997, 1: 19–24.

Restuccia, D., and Rogerson, R. Policy Distortions and Aggregate Productivity With Heterogeneous Establishments. *Review of Economic Dynamics*, 2008, 11(4): 707–720.

Romer, P. M. Endogenous Technological Change. *Journal of Political Economy*, 1990, XCVIII: S71–S102.

Romer, P. M. Human Capital and Growth: Theory and Evidence. *Carnegie-Rochester Conference Series on Public Policy*. North-Holland, 1990, 32: 251–286.

Shi, Q. Q., Qin, B. T., and Chen, J. *Technological Progress and Economic Growth*. Beijing, Science and Technology Literature Press (in Chinese), 1985.

Solow, R. M. Technical Change and the Aggregate Production Function. *The Review of Economics and Statistics*, 1957, 39(3): 312–320.

Tinbergen, J. Zur Theorie der langfristigen Wirtschaftsentwicklung (On the Theory of Long-term Economic Growth). *WeltwirtschaftlichesArchiv*, 1942, 55. Bd.: 511–549.

Wang, X. L., Fan, G., and Liu, P. Pattern and Sustainability of China's Economic Growth towards 2020 [R]. CEDRI Working Paper, 2007. Available at http://cerdi. org/uploads/sfCmsContent/html/203/FanGang_alii.pdf.

Wei, X. H., and Zhang, J. W. Threshold Effect of Human Capital on TFP Growth: Evidence From China. *Chinese Journal of Population Science* (in Chinese), 2010, 5: 48–57.

Wooldridge, J. M. *Introductory Econometrics: A Modern Approach* (2nd Edition). Cincinnati, OH, South-Western, Division of Thomson Learning, 2003.

The World Bank. *Growth in the Post-Crisis Global Economy: Policy Challenges for Developing Countries*. Development Committee of the Board of Governors of the World Bank and the IMF, Washington, DC: March, 2014. Available at http://site resources.worldbank.org/EXTPREMNET/Resources/489960-1338997241035/ Growth_Commission_Special_Report.pdf

The joint research group of the World Bank and the Development Research Center of the State Council. In *China in 2030: Building a Modernized Harmonious and Creative Society*. Beijing: China Financial and Economic Publishing House, 2013.

Zhang, J., Wu, G. Y., and Zhang, J. P. The Estimation of China's Provincial Capital Stock: 1952–2000. *Economic Research Journal* (in Chinese), 2004, 10: 35–44.

Zhang, J., and Zhang, Y. Recalculating the Capital of China and a Review of Li and Tang's Article. *Economic Research Journal* (in Chinese), 2003, 7: 35–43.

Zhang, Y. Q. China's Productivity: Past Success and Future Challenges. MPFD Working Paper no. WP/16/06, 2016. Bangkok: ESCAP. Available at www.unes cap.org/publications.

Zhang, Y. Q., and Lou, F. Analysis and Forecast on the Potential of China's Economic Growth. *The Journal of Quantitative & Technical Economics* (in Chinese), 2009, 12: 137–145.

Zhuang, J. Z., Vandenberg, P., and Huang, Y. P. *Growing Beyond the Low-Cost Advantage: How the People's Republic of China Can Avoid the Middle-Income Trap? [R]*. Manila and Beijing, Asian Development Bank and Peking University, 2012.

Index

78   *Index*